MAKING GROWTH HAPPEN

MAKING GROWTH HAPPEN
Learning from First-Generation Entrepreneurs

S.J. Phansalkar

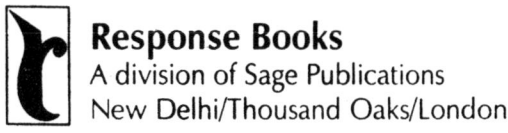

Response Books
A division of Sage Publications
New Delhi/Thousand Oaks/London

Copyright © S.J. Phansalkar and National Dairy Development Board, Anand, 1999

All rights reserved. No part of this book may be reproduced or utilised in any form or by any means, electronic or mechanical, including photocopying, recording or by any information storage or retrieval system, without permission in writing from the publisher.

First published in 1999 by

Response Books
A division of Sage Publications India Pvt Ltd
32 M–Block Market, Greater Kailash–I
New Delhi 110 048

Sage Publications Inc
2455 Teller Road
Thousand Oaks, California 91320

Sage Publications Ltd
6 Bonhill Street
London EC2A 4PU

Published by Tejeshwar Singh for Response Books, lasertypeset by Line Arts, Pondicherry and printed at Chaman Enterprises, Darya Ganj, New Delhi 110 002.

The views expressed and statements made in this book are the sole responsibility of the author, Dr S.J. Phansalkar. The National Dairy Development Board shall in no way be held directly or indirectly responsible for these views.

Library of Congress Cataloging-in-Publication Data
Phansalkar, S.J. (Sanjiv Janardan)
  Making growth happen: learning from first-generation entrepreneurs/ S.J. Phansalkar.
    p. cm.   (cloth: alk. paper)   (pbk.: alk. paper)
  1. Entrepreneurship—India. 2. Success in business—India. 3. Business-people—India. 4. Entrepreneurship. 5. Success in business. 6. Business-people. I. Title.

HB615.P397   658.4′21′0954—dc21   1998   98–37063

ISBN: 0–7619–9293–6 (US-Hb)   81–7036–756–5 (India-Hb)
      0–7619–9294–4 (US-Pb)   81–7036–757–3 (India-Pb)

Production Team: Anita Misra, R.A.M. Brown and Santosh Rawat

To
Dr V Kurien
former Chairman, NDDB, Anand,
who pioneered the growth of not just one enterprise but a whole sector of the economy

To
Dr V Kurien
Chairman, NDDB, Anand
who pleaded to do so with us not just our enterprise
but a whole sector of the economy

Contents

List of Abbreviations	9
Preface	11
Acknowledgements	15
1. Introduction	17
2. The Successful Companies Studied	31
3. Learning from Success: An Illustration of a Case and its Analysis	69
4. Marketing in the Successful Companies	105
5. Managing Money: Financial Strategies of the Successful Companies	125
6. Manufacturing and Logistics in the Successful Companies	141
7. Organisational Issues and Management Styles	161
8. Management of Human Resources in the Successful Companies	179
9. So What is New in the Management of the Successful Companies?	189
10. Strategies Adopted by the Successful Companies	199
About the Author	231

List of Abbreviations

AMC	Annual Maintenance Contract
CA	Chartered Accountant
CHC	Closely Held Company
CEO	Chief Executive Officer
COO	Chief Operating Officer
CSIR	Council for Scientific and Industrial Research
DPCO	Drugs Price Control Order
DRL	Dr Reddy's Laboratories
EOU	Export Oriented Unit
ESOP	Employees Stock Option
ETP	Effluent Treatment Plant
FMCG	Fast-Moving Consumer Goods
GIDC	Gujarat Industrial Development Corporation
GP	General Practitioner
HRD	Human Resource Development
IPO	Initial Public Offer
IT	Information Technology
MD	Managing Director
MIS	Management Information System
MNC	Multinational Company
NASSCOM	National Association of Software and Service Companies (New Delhi)

NDDB	National Dairy Development Board
PLC	Product Life Cycle
PSR	Professional Service Representative
PSU	Public Sector Undertaking
QA	Quality Assurance
QC	Quality Circle
RB	Rice Bran
RDBMS	Relational Database Management System
REC	Regional Engineering College
SE	Solvent Extraction
SEEPZ	Santacruz Electronics Export Promotion Zone
SME	Small and Medium Enterprises
SSI	Small-scale Industry
TDICI	Technology Development and Investment Corporation of India
USP	Unique Selling Proposition
WHC	Widely Held Company

Preface

Several strands of thought led to the idea of writing this book and the research that preceded it. In the first place, mild suggestions from my professional colleagues that my book (*How Not to Ruin Your Small Industry*, Response, 1996) which preceded this was a shade one-sided and focused only on wrong managerial actions, made me think of the need to study and write on successes. During my various training programmes for corporate managers, this issue of not being able to give positive examples but being restricted to talking only of wrong actions of management emphasised this need. The research provided a very rich opportunity to learn about managerial action in well-managed companies.

For too long have management professors in India taught cases from the US and Europe. The heroes about whom students are told are all from the US, Japan or Europe. Here an Iacocca, there a Matsushita, though no doubt worthy fellows, all of them. Partly I suppose because the professors themselves, poor fellows, studied in the West and partly because not too much casework is undertaken in this country. As I argued in my last book, most Indian small industries must grow big merely in order to survive. With little documentation of Indian companies, how is one to talk to them about growth in the Indian economic environment? Surely not just by giving examples of Bill Gates and Rupert Murdoch. I think it is thus imperative to recognise Indian heroes (and of course, heroines) of the industrial world, to study their actions and decisions, to learn from them, to write about them and to document their strategies. After all, India is at the threshold of becoming a global economic player. And the sooner we learn to take pride in our industrial pioneers, the better it will be for all of us.

Given the occidental leaning of management academics, not unnaturally, during hundreds of discussions with the homegrown businessman, I have heard that 'all this management theory is not applicable to Indian business'. I am by nature somewhat submissive and the typical Indian businessman by nature tends to be more than somewhat aggressive. I do hold forth in front of elite audience and large classrooms full of senior corporate managers. And yet I tend to listen respectfully, if not with rapt attention, to the stagnant-water pugilists' wisdom of the rugged backyard industrialist or the slightly shifty, overgrown petty trader. Nevertheless, repeated assertions like this by scores of homegrown businessmen had their effect. They almost made me feel guilty about living off the fat of the land despite being educated only in the 'Western management theories'. Anyhow, I always had this somewhat idle curiosity to find out whether successful Indian businesses behaved in ways that so-called 'Western management theory' would expect or did something dramatically different. The only trouble is, I have too much concern for probity to regard every gold-toothed Indian mogul as a successful businessman worthy of study and respect.

Finally, there was a very powerful motive arising out of a rather limited worldview. In management academics, the professor undertaking consulting assignments is a recognised figure. But a self-employed management consultant undertaking research is uncommon. So when the National Dairy Development Board (NDDB) agreed to finance this research, I was very gratified. Here I was, a self-employed person undertaking research work that a professor of any management institute should have been happy to engage in. There is no harm in occasionally feeling a bit smug.

Be that as it may, I think I have something to say that will be of use to those who manage enterprises and dream of growing big. And I am sure that students of management as well as their stern professors will find examples of managerial action in well-managed companies from which they can learn a lot. And if the reviews of and feedback on this book turn out like those on the first one, I can be counted upon to come up with another in not too distant a future!

S.J. Phansalkar

Acknowledgements

The National Dairy Development Board, Anand, gave a very generous grant that enabled me to do the research on which this book is based, and also to make the two ends meet. I am deeply thankful to them for the support and trust given by them.

Chief executives and senior managers of the companies studied permitted me and my colleagues access to their data, personnel and facilities to make case writing possible. They also offered valuable comments on the cases themselves and on the first draft of the manuscript sent to them. I am indebted to them for their kind help.

Many friends, but notably Sarvashri Malcolm Harper, R. Srinivasan, Vijay Mahajan, C. Balaji, P. Durgaprasad, Debiprasad Mishra, Samir Barua and M.S. Sriram encouraged and helped me in conceptualising and carrying out the research. I am grateful to them.

Sarvashri Ajit Kanitkar, Shyamal Gupta, P.T. Pradeep, Vivekanand Shenoy and Kuldip Singh, and Ms Sheela and Sudeshna Mukharji collaborated with me during this research. Shyamal also assisted in preparation of the documents. I thank them for their scholarly and prompt work.

R. Srinivasan and Ajit Kanitkar allowed me to trespass on their goodwill and make them read and comment on the initial drafts of this book. Much improvement in the first draft is due to their suggestions and comments. Such shortcomings as may be detected in the book are, of course, my doing.

Many other persons, too numerous to mention, helped me during the research and writing process in a variety of ways. I am grateful to all of them.

Finally, I thank my dear wife for encouraging me in this work.

S.J.P.

1

Introduction

How This Book Came About

I wrote the book titled *How Not to Ruin Your Small Industry* (Response, 1996) about two years back. That was based on my numerous, though unstructured, interactions with small-industry owners. Also on my observations about the SSI sector when I sought consulting work in it. That book focused on several categories of inappropriate managerial actions which I rather emphatically called 'blunders'. These blunders keep the industrial unit stagnant and can possibly make it sick as well.

The inappropriate managerial actions which I call blunders are:

- excessive dependence on one buyer
- expanding fixed asset base without providing for enough working capital
- speculating on borrowed money
- doing informal business
- floating too many firms
- marketing myopia

- hiring persons for reasons other than their competence
- unrealistic project planning

In my subsequent interactions with hundreds of entrepreneurs, it appeared that most of them were familiar with these acts and quite a few had suffered from their consequences. Across regions of the country and sectors of the economy. The SSI ethos, it seems, makes it difficult to not commit these blunders. Obviously, my perspicacity made me rather pensive and sad. Whenever I use the term blunders in the following text, I refer to some of these acts.

The harried entrepreneurs are usually very hard-pressed in trying to keep the sales going up, the payments coming in and the officers from myriad departments smiling indulgently. Seldom do they want or seriously take the advice of a general management consultant. For he offers no quick-fix solutions to their common maladies. He speaks of the mindset of the small industry owner, patterns of decision making and esoterica of that sort. Exhortations of good habits are much less welcome than curative medicines and sure fire 'Down ten kilos in three weeks' exercises, as most chronic patients will vouch. The same is true of entrepreneurs. The general management guy talks about what the entrepreneur feels he knows any way. And it does not immediately redress his working capital, labour law, pollution or sales tax case. So why worry? So the book did not bring in more consulting from the small industry sector!

Possibly the entrepreneurs and myself, both have benefited from the fact that the SSI sector gave me no consulting but merely ideas about that book! Many kind words were spoken and written about it by many industrialists and even otherwise stern academics. One worthy industrialist-turned-teacher went to the extent of saying that every small-scale industrialist must read it. I admire such friendly sentiments, particularly if they are going to keep the sales figures pushing! The upshot, of course, is that I am back with another one. Hopefully a little more helpful about what to do this time. And not merely what to avoid. But there is a marked difference now. I have actually spent a lot of time deliberately studying the subject matter before writing this one. So the reader will pardon me if I take it seriously. And I want the reader to take it even more seriously than the first book.

It is all right, I was told, to claim that some decisions are blunders, but what if every one—including the very successful ones—also committed them? Would I not then be guilty of barking up the wrong tree? Of finding fault with the management of small enterprises when actually the environment was to be blamed solely? Of telling the entrepreneurs that they were blundering, unthinking, myopic managers when they were plain unfortunate? Was I mixing up the incompetent with the unfortunate? Did the lucky ones manage to blunder their way out of blunders and were the unlucky ones forced to lick their wounds? Hence I was advised by some of my professional colleagues that it might be worthwhile to look at how some of the very successful companies had grown. That it might be better if one looked at companies started by folks who were ordinary when they started them. The best way to do this was to find out by researching.

About the Case Research on Successful Enterprises

Undertaking research is expensive. I was fortunate when NDDB kindly agreed to fund my research through a very generous research grant. I undertook this research during 1997. Three colleagues helped me in the process. The research was targeted at finding out whether there were certain similar things which successful entrepreneurs all do, whether there are commonalities in their efforts to grow, whether their management practices differ from those of the blunderers and if so, how. It was an exploratory research by design. By that I mean that I did not begin with a specific hypothesis which I wanted to prove.

NDDB had desired me to focus on the agro-processing units. That would have been of some assistance to them and to the many agro-processing cooperatives whom the Board supports, and I too would have been able to meet my research objective to a substantial extent. What happened was something else again. It emerged that there just are not that many successful agro-businesses worthy of study in this country. And fewer still whose management practices deserve to be emulated. And of those few that were judged to be successfully and soundly managed, some would not let me in.

So I studied successful companies in other sectors. I' had committed to NDDB that I would do 12 cases in one year, the period for which the research grant was made. It took me 15 months to complete the cases. I tried to look at successful companies. It emerged after much literature review and discussions with professional colleagues that several things would need to be carefully thought through. After all, how was one to define success? Should one study multinational subsidiaries? Companies floated half a century back? Companies floated by the sons of the industrial patrons? Cooperatives? That brought me back to the primary purpose of the research. It was born out of the desire to build on what I had written in *How Not to Ruin Your Small Industry*. Hence it was more important to look at companies set up by first-generation entrepreneurs, companies that had successfully grown out of the small-industry status. And companies that had done so in a relatively recent past.

I made my operative definition of 'candidate companies' as

- those started by first generation entrepreneurs
- those that began after 1975 or thereabout
- those that crossed a turnover of Rs 300 million (or equivalent) in a decade or at least became recognised success stories in their product lines, and are continuing to do well till date

- those whom the market, customers and investment community held in good regard (with no whispers about money laundering, siphoning of funds, cheating the investors, massive *hawala*-type operations or other forms of commercial misdemeanour about them)

I do not know whether any one of you did case research in the corporate world in India. Those of you who did will agree that it is a tough proposition. Access to companies is difficult. A business journalist or an equity analyst is a fairly common entity but a management case researcher does not seem to be. Companies seldom want researchers who do not owe them any allegiance to come and ask their managers and staff all sorts of questions. Transparency and openness apart, there is also the question of sparing the time of their staff. This is quite natural. After all, in our daily lives we do not want absolute strangers to prowl about our homes. If he comes with good credentials, we do welcome him in our drawing room and act the polite hosts to him. But he cannot move freely in our homes and ask what he will to everyone. The outside researcher is at times viewed as a pain. Thus while I should have taken a very objective database to select my sample and gone ahead only on that basis, things became more difficult.

To begin with, I did identify a list of successful companies which met my criteria. That is quite easy these days when good companies like CMIE and others give you sound databases. After identifying successes on financial scores alone, I went around finding out about them to see whether they were smelly. I found at least four dozen successful, well-managed and 'thoroughly respectable' companies. So I wrote to them. However, I got access to very few on this basis. And in two companies where my colleague and I did gain access on this basis, we were kicked out after investing a lot of our time and money. An excise raid finished one effort while a political agitation saw the end of the other.

Of course I could not just fold my hands and write an armchair book. So then I pressed the second strategy in action:

figuring out whom one knows and whether he can put you in touch with the key actors in some successful company. Access to interviews, data and people is granted only if you know the CEO well and he trusts you. Unfortunately I do not know many exceptionally successful CEOs. So access had to be gained through friends. This could be tricky. Having persuaded a company to provide access to its data, if one discovered that it did not really meet the criteria, what was one to do? Such issues had to be tackled.

Thus while I can honestly say that I have not compromised on the selection criteria, I must admit that there are quite a few companies that met the above criteria which I had approached but are not covered in this study. Nevertheless, most of the companies discussed in this book are very well managed, are remarkable successes and offer valuable lessons to entrepreneurs who wish to know what to do. That is what counts.

What does This Book Contain?

We studied 10 companies, namely Ashima Syntex Limited, Biocon India Limited, Doctor Reddy's Laboratories Limited, Mastek Limited, Praj Industries Limited, Sudha Oils and Chemical Industries Limited, Orchid Chemicals and Pharmaceuticals Limited, Sun Pharmaceutical Industries Limited, Sumangal Prakashan (P) Limited and V-Guard Industries Limited. I have prepared formal cases on these companies that can be used as teaching instruments. Teachers desiring to use them can write to me for copies. These cases have clearance from the companies for publication and use in academic fora. Inclusion of the full cases would have made this book bulkier and costlier. I have therefore presented the summaries of the cases in Chapter 2, as also one full case with its analysis in Chapter 3 so as to illustrate the research process and the logic of my arguments. This is because many of the things that follow become clear only when at least one case analysis is fully illustrated.

Not all the inferences drawn here need meet with complete agreement of the management of these companies. That is an irrelevant matter. So long as I am faithful to facts, the interpretation is my responsibility. Having analysed the cases and inferred in good faith, their agreement with it can only be a matter of idle curiosity. I will also be bringing in the lessons learnt from some of the other successful companies whenever the occasion arises.

The subsequent five chapters discuss the noteworthy features of the management practices in these successful companies. These are arranged by functional area. The innovative or uncommon things done by these companies and how these relate to their business success are discussed in Chapter 9. I revert to general management issues and the lessons learnt from the research in the last chapter.

I would like to emphasise that this book is meant for practitioners. Though most of its material is from research, it is written much more informally than a research report. Throughout, I write in first person singular and in an informal language. While most of the points I have made in this book are based on my research, I will quote the instance of a company only when I think that a particular point deserves to be illustrated with the help of a specific example from my research. Whenever I am drawing inferences of a conceptual type, I will try to take the reader along by relating the actions to management theory.

The Story in Brief

Some readers cannot wait to read through all the pages of a mystery novel, but want to know whodunit in the first para itself. This research is about strategies and processes. Even so, many impatient readers—management students in particular—will want to know the conclusions quickly. (Management students open a book and wish to get something which they can quickly quote somewhere, and often just because it sounds good!) For such impatient souls, and always hoping that having so quoted they will then care to read the rest of the book just to see if they have quoted out of context, what the book talks about is as follows. This might also assist others in making up their minds as to whether to go on at all.

The story in brief is as follows:

- Companies that began small and succeeded in transiting to medium scale did not try their hand in every conceivable thing. They identified their line carefully and stuck to it. They grew in it, usually by selling harder and over a wider area. Some of them also introduced product lines that were extensions of their existing lines. They worked hard to learn how to produce products of high quality and at a lower cost. Their mastery over the technology of production or an innovative operating technology (for meaning of this, see Chapter 6) was their main strength and this strength they tried to exploit while growing or selecting alternate lines of business.
- The simplest way to grow is to take up in the first place a product line the market for which is itself growing when one starts the enterprise. This does run counter to the usual tendency to take up something established—a *chalnewala* item, as a Marwari friend of mine put it. Second, the core of the enterprise's competitive strength is in making a good product, one that offers features of use and relevance to the buyers. Constant focus on improving product features and keeping consistent quality is thus very important to growth and success. Finally, in this country where value-for-money dominates consumer behaviour, companies must learn to take a price position that is competitive. Taxes and duties form a substantial proportion of the price that a consumer pays.

Often it is tempting to do informal business to avoid paying these and thus achieving a competitive price position. Quite a few small industry units do it. If a competitive price position is to be taken without doing such 'informal business', companies must learn to control their costs.

- The finance story is counter-intuitive. The bold, it seems, is not very beautiful. Excessive leveraging by heavy borrowings, a common trait of the businessman who is in a hurry and at times not desirous of repaying his debts, is never conducive to growth. Some entrepreneurs do it since their financial muscle falls short of their growth ambition, but then they must bring down the debt as quickly as possible. Second, it is important to build up a solid liquidity position and raise the level of current assets. Follow the trade norms for inventory in the market and for trade credits but cut down working capital need everywhere else, seems to be the best policy to pursue. Blocking all one's money in frozen assets is the most important thing to avoid. Those who defy these golden principles of conservative finance may show brilliant performance but only for a while, before they bust up.

- But what is most revealing is the basic strength behind the success of every company studied. Companies that become big and successful often start very small. In a backyard may be. They try to keep the size of the manufacturing facility just right for the sales they expect in the current year or the next. And they expand slowly, but steadily. But all the time they are bootstrapping, trying to make little changes in manufacturing or logistics of purchase, storage and transport. All such changes contribute to reducing their cost of manufacturing and yet steadily improving or at least consistently maintaining the quality of their products. Such low cost yet superior quality positions naturally help them hold the price line without compromising on quality.

- Each one of the companies studied had innovated in some way or the other. But entrepreneurs are not inventors. So they innovate not new products or technologies but newer ways of doing things—of managing manufacturing or making a sales pitch or eliminating water shortage or structuring themselves, etc. Possibly, they may not be the first to adopt these new things, but they certainly are among the few who do it. By discovering a new way of doing things, they develop a competitive weapon only they have. These innovations might be forced on them by circumstances, but as one entrepreneur stated, 'I had a lot of time then (when his innovations evolved) but little money and hence I had to use my time in designing things, and this worked.'
- Finally there is the question of the mind. Most successful companies try to transit to becoming public limited companies. In India, becoming public has come to mean being able to extract money from the gullible small investors. That is how even companies with issue ratings below 35 also went public. Becoming widely held for these reasons was not the intention of any of the successful companies. In fact, in most of these companies, key promoters have maintained their stake at high levels—in one case at a whopping 73 per cent. I am talking about virtues of becoming public limited in terms of the attendent management style. There is a major advantage in the need to become formal, structured and accountable. The successful companies found the 'small industrialist mindset'—the typical gray-zone mentality of the faceless SSI owner—far too restrictive to facilitate growth. Having become public limited companies, the entrepreneurs learnt to give up their excessive possessiveness about the enterprise. They realised that the world is too complex for them to revel in their omniscience. They required and hence hired professionals, possibly at fat salaries. They needed and hence encouraged their

colleagues and senior staff to participate in a team effort. Their earlier peremptory authority to make decisions was replaced with open, transparent, formal and structured organisational processes. They did not continue to feel that they required people to work for *them* as *individuals*, but for *their companies* as *organisations*. This difference is crucial and if an entrepreneur does not understand its significance, he will not grow to become an industrial giant.

So that is the story. No, the earth is not shaking, nor did I set out to shake it. I suggest that the reader also tries to read between the lines to see what is not covered in the findings.

Disclaimers

In the first place, the cases are from among a much larger set of successful companies. Hence it is possible that one may have missed out on some factors that could be associated with successful enterprises in the country. I really do not claim a universal validity of the points that come about, rather the utility of these lessons. Hypotheses are developed here, rather than proved. Some day, hopefully, someone else will give me another grant to test these hypotheses.

The second disclaimer is important too. An interesting book which is also based on case research argues that if you look at only successful or excellent companies for factors leading to success, then you might come to associate things common to them but not unique to successful companies. You might for example discover that they all had well-designed buildings, posh offices, charming receptionists, etc. And since these are commonly found in successful companies, you might say that posh offices and charming receptionists lead to success. (Those interested may read 'Built to Last', by James C. Collins and Jerry I. Porras, *Harper Business*,

New York, 1994). I have looked at only successes. Am I then reporting only buildings and charming receptionists? I should hope not. I suspect that while one may not have demonstrable evidence of it, I have tried to bring out only those features that I never found in the hundreds of enterprises which are stagnant and sick. In fact, what is common to them—*the failures*—has been documented in my earlier book. Whether the successful ones also did those things is discussed in Chapter 7. So I hope to have brought out the factors for success other than buildings and charming receptionists.

A Digression on Agro-business in India

As I mentioned earlier, the agro-business sector was to have given me most of the cases. I found it difficult to locate the requisite number of companies worthy of study. One reason was the fact that the proportion of 'gray zone' business is much higher in agro-business. There are many other reasons why there are not so many long-term successes in it. To complete the story of my research, I add a digression on why the agro-business sector has not been a sector of thumpingly successful enterprises as it was expected to be. Those who are not interested in agro-business nor wish to start a business on their grandfather's farm can skip this. I do offer some reasons for the fact that there are few long-term successes in agro-businesses post-1970s.

Indian foods and agro-business in general face a situation characterised by the following set of factors:

- Absence of mechanised processes for making typical Indian foods on a large scale in ways which are obviously superior to traditional methods. This means the industrialist in this line may grow by managing a constellation of small-capacity units spread all over. This introduces the problem of uniformity of quality.

- Fragmented production system of the underlying commodity. This fragmentation makes large-scale processing possible only if one develops quality-preserving logistics of transport and multiple point storage. The successful agro-businesses are only in those commodities that have compact and rich command areas, such as soyabean.
- Poorly developed marketing, storage and transportation systems, which makes the development of quality-preserving logistics very difficult.
- Severe and multiple regulations on procurement, movement, processing and sales of commodities and products under state and central legislations. These make the task of expanding in these lines horrendously problem ridden, putting premium on small size.
- Prevalence of complex, multipoint and corrupt fiscal regime which nurtures the gray zone at the cost of the formal and honest sector.

The last two features favour gray-zone behaviour and facelessness. It is facile to operate in a commercial gray zone if one has a unit which has a small capacity, is producing hopelessly traditional products and is selling without a strong market presence in terms of brand equity. That way one remains faceless and can escape many of the laws unnoticed. The total cost of abiding by/managing the various laws, regulations and types of taxes relevant to an agro-processing unit (to list but a few, the Essential Commodities Act, Weights and Measures Act, Prevention of Food Adulteration Act, etc; small-industry reservations and commodity-specific state-level regulations, e.g., on sugarcane, certain oil seeds and pulses; and in terms of taxes the mandi tax, purchase tax, turnover tax, the differential sales tax rates and so on) generally exceeds 10 per cent of the value of the sales. That being smaller than the effective margin (agro-processing businesses are, at best, marginal value-addition businesses, with raw material accounting for upwards of 75 per cent of the costs, processing accounting for about 12–15 per cent and the balance being taxation and margins), the faceless operator is in a superior position to compete. Thus the agro-processing sector appears to have strong diseconomies of scale as of the moment.

In consequence, not too many entrepreneurs have grown big. Quite a few of those who did possibly did so by doing what I consider wrong things, such as thriving in the gray zone, floating too many firms, outright manipulation of laws, and so on. So while the sector might produce wealth, more likely it is the individuals' unaccounted wealth rather than investible and growth-oriented industrial wealth. There are of course a few honourable exceptions. Only when the advantages of the superior technology are so strong as to outweigh the advantages of facelessness, can the large operator compete. Provided of course that there is enough market for the modern products which he makes. That exists readily only for products suiting the unique Indian palate. Or else there is the huge overhead of having to promote and market the new product, which is more for people like Nestles and seldom possible for a small entrepreneur. Thus the scope for successful agro-processing units is really restricted to that segment which can go to scale using distinctly superior technology, at the same time catering to Indian needs and demand.

2

The Successful Companies Studied

I myself conducted the case research in seven companies. Ajit Kanitkar and Shyamal Gupta studied two each and a team of three—Pradeep, Sheela and Vivekanand from Kochi—wrote one case study. Of these 12, I have used 10 for this book, while the other two were dropped for collateral reasons. The cases used in this book are on the companies listed in the first chapter. Some basic details about these companies are given below.

Sl. No.	Name of the Company	Business	Location
1	Sun Pharmaceutical	Healthcare	Baroda/Mumbai
2	Dr Reddy's Lab	Healthcare	Hyderabad
3	Orchid Chemicals	Healthcare	Chennai
4	Biocon Ltd	Enzymes	Bangalore
5	Mastek Ltd	Software	Mumbai
6	Sumangal Prakashan	Calendars	Mumbai
7	Praj Industries	Distillery/Brewery, Process Equipment and Systems	Pune

Sl. No.	Name of the Company	Business	Location
8	V-Guard Industries	Voltage Stabilisers	Cochin
9	Ashima Syntex	Textiles	Ahmedabad
10	Sudha Agro-Oils & Chemical Ind.	Rice Bran Oil	Samalkot

General Information on the Companies

The oldest among these companies was Sumangal Prakashan (1973) and the youngest Orchid (1993). Marketmen and observers of business were in general very positive about all the companies, some highly sought after by the foreign institutional investors. TDICI had taken interest in four of these. Though financing by TDICI was not a consideration, it is generally believed that TDICI looks at proposals very seriously and picks up winners. There was no talk about absence of probity or underhand deals in any of the companies. Their turnover for 1995–97 ranged between Rs 200 million (in case of Sumangal—even then we chose it because it is the recognised leader in the almanac-cum-calendar line in the country) to Rs 2120 million. All these companies started as single-product, single-facility companies, but most now have greater complexity in terms of products, facilities and technologies. The companies started mostly with the same activities they are currently known for or took them up shortly after experimenting with other lines.

It was not possible for me to get the 'industry standards' or benchmarks of performance for the companies studied. In fact, the business of some of the companies is too specialised to make any comparison meaningful. However, wherever appropriate and available, I have given some key indicators of financial performance for the industry alongside those for the company being discussed.

Sl. No.	Ratio	Pharma Industry	DRL	Sun	Orchid+	Software	Mastek	Cotton Tex.	Ashima	Oil	Sudha
1	Debt-Equity Ratio	0.97	0.04	0.16	0.37	0.58	0.49	3.77	1.07	1.128	2.069
2	Gross Margin/Sales (%)	14.4	21	23	14	16.8	19	12.3	13	5.5	4
3	Wage Cost/Sales (%)	6.3	5	5	1	6.1	19	7.7	1	1.5	1
4	Advertising and Mktg. Expenses/Sales (%)	5.9	0.28*	8.17**	0.2	2.9	0.05	2.5	0.05	1.3	0.05
5	Depreciation/Sales (%)	2.6	9	2	3.2	2.4	13	2	7.9	1	7.9
6	Inventory Turnover (Days)	68	83	56	99	NA	NA	68	67	24.29	67
7	Debtors (Days)	56	118	65	3	93	169	47	17	23	17
8	Working Capital as % of CE	NA	0.03	0.04	0.01	NA	3.2	NA	0.03	NA	0.018
9	R&D Expenses/Sales (%)		5.14	3.62	0.62	NA	NA	NA	NA	NA	NA

All the figures are for 1994–95.
* For the year 1995–96.
** Selling and distribution expenses included.
+ 1995–96 figure.

Sun Pharmaceuticals Industries Ltd

(Case prepared by S.J. Phansalkar)
(Established 1978, Turnover (1997) Rs 160 crore)

Dilip Shanghvi started a small pharmaceutical formulations unit in 1982 at Vapi, with three business partners. Prior to that, he was operating from Calcutta where he marketed certain psychotropic drugs (tranquillisers and other medicines used in psychotherapy), formulated on loan license basis in third-party facilities around Calcutta.

Sun grew steadily at first by remaining a single-therapy company. The Vapi facility was expanded twice as the product line widened within the therapy. A group company called Unimed set up facilities at Halol and Sun marketed its products as well. Sun entered cardio-vascular therapy in 1988. It also started marketing drugs for gastro-enteritis problems. In 1990, after crossing a turnover of Rs one crore per year, it started shedding the small-industry image. This was done by vesting the business of the firm (till then a partnership) in the present company by operation of the law. Sun set up a modern R&D centre in 1993 inaugurated by the Vice-President of India. The centre concerns itself with product as well as process research. Sun's maiden public issue in 1994 was massively oversubscribed and brought a lot of liquid cash to the group.

Aside from expanding and consolidating its manufacturing facilities, the company started acquiring business firms to further increase its market share and presence. The company has till now acquired controlling interests in three Indian companies, bought the manufacturing unit of one more and set up one overseas subsidiary in the US producing generic medicines. It also exports to many other countries.

As Dilip Shanghvi says, initially he had a lot of time and very little money. He used his time well and devised some very innovative marketing strategies. These included making deliberate and sustained efforts at creating a special image of the company; creating goodwill among practitioners by innovating on Continuing Education Programmes with the collaboration of local chapters of the Indian Medical Association (IMA); providing rare, recent and current books and monographs on medical problems of concern to doctors as gifts; etc. Sun also took exceptional care in ensuring high product quality. At the same time, it grew in partnership with vendors and suppliers. Today Dilip Shanghvi has somewhat more money but little time. The company has therefore evolved structures and systems for decentralising the decision-initiation and -making processes. It grows by design, by buying up facilities or by acquiring majority stake in companies by paying cash, because 'Sun equity is very precious'.

Sun's growth should offer lessons to every entrepreneur: patience, hard work, optimising on efforts and conservative financing. Shanghvi borrowed from family friends and others, but these borrowings were preferred for ease of access and were never for speculative purposes. The tactics of operating many firms for a limited purpose ensured flexibility but Sun's turnover and profits did not suffer for it. His employee- as well as vendor-relations policies are commendable. Above all, it is the innovative marketing strategy of Sun which offers the wisdom to use your time and energies in thinking up plans and strategies that can assist your growth even if you do not have much money.

Dr Reddy's Laboratories (DRL)

(Case prepared by S.J. Phansalkar)
(Established 1984, Turnover (1997) Rs 252 crore)

(Uniloids, Dr Anji Reddy's first venture, was established in 1973 and Standard Organics in 1979. Dr Reddy's Laboratory is thus his third venture, though he is a first generation entrepreneur.)

Profit & Loss Account of Sun

Rs lakh

	1990	1991	1992	1993	1994	1995	1996
Sales	972	1457	2459	3138	5131	9211	13017
Other Income	2	9	54	87	115	174	89
Materials	423	619	1202	1625	2649	4259	5120
Excise	127	169	210	257	282	915	1349
Personnel	66	93	151	238	328	557	788
Operating Cost	243	396	534	662	1004	1355	1870
Interest	11	17	60	111	128	0	0
Depreciation	13	37	13	19	35	117	279
PBT	91	135	343	313	820	2179	3697
Tax	0	0	35	61	82	35	0
Adjustments	0	0	31	1	6	0	0
PAT	91	135	339	253	744	2144	2179

Source: Prospectus issued in 1994 and Annual Reports thereafter

Condensed Balance Sheets of Sun as on 31 March

Rs lakh

	1993	1994	1995	1996
Share Capital	641	719	1476	1480
(Incl. of bal. in Shareholders' A/c)				
Reserves	28	956	7902	11284
Secured Loans	641	1478	1476	1761
Unsecured Loans	211	223	53	48
Current Liabilities & Provisions	394	1001	1669	2354
Total	1785	4377	12576	16927
Gross Block	676	1861	3692	5856
Depreciation	53	888	205	483
Net Block	623	1773	3486	5260
CWIP	11	220	29	0.15
Investments	2	2	319	727
Inventories	524	1057	1333	3030
Debtors	560	742	1541	2036
Cash & Bank	24	127	527	263
Deferred Expenses			87	59
Loans and Advances	171	456	5254	5549

Source: Prospectus issued in 1994 and Annual Reports thereafter
Note: Figures have been rounded off.

Dr Anji Reddy, a chemical engineer, joined the Indian Drugs and Pharmaceuticals Ltd (IDPL) in 1967. He worked in the chief technologist's team at IDPL. This team had the mandate of ensuring that the laboratory-level technologies developed by the scientists were actually deployed in the manufacturing facilities. After working for a few years in IDPL, he went on his own in 1974. Uniloids was set up for producing a drug hitherto imported. His technical skill and ability to identify opportunities in the pharma line saw his firm growing. Another company, Standard Organics Limited, was formed five years later in partnership with one of his friends. The firm Dr Reddy's Laboratories followed in 1984, almost a decade after he started his own business. He separated from his partner as they did not share the same vision.

Anji Reddy started numerous firms around the mid-1980s: a lease finance company to garner public resources, two drug companies which have survived and grown big, one computer peripherals manufacturing company, etc. But the focus was clearly on the pharma line. He relied on his own personal talent in identifying business opportunities in the line. The criteria for choosing new products for DRL appear to have been (a) the absence of DPCO influence, (b) the possibility of producing a drug without violating the Indian Patents' Act (which recognises only process patents), and (c) the ability to quickly expand production before other manufacturers followed suit. This strategy was adopted time and again. DRL's most dramatic success was achieved with the drug Quinolones in the late 1980s. Its sister company Cheminor manufactured Ibuprofen, again for a similar set of reasons.

If Anji Reddy was a trifle adventurous with his financing methods—loans, GDRs and public issues, he was positively daring with the application of funds. His most courageous decision was to invest heavily in his research foundation. That investment has now more than paid for itself as it has developed more than 25 original products for which it has filed patents in the US. One of these drugs, a medicine to be used in diabetes therapy, has been given to a European company on royalty, the proceeds of which will be truly amazing.

The company set up a 100 per cent EOU for manufacturing halogen lamps. This somewhat tangential investment was done to reap the advantages of fiscal laws. The company built up its standing and muscle on bulk-drugs business. The bulk drugs made by them were always cheaper and more accessible than the import operations. They always ensured high quality production. With the availability of a cheaper domestic bulk drug, many formulators would start selling the medicines. This would create large demand and bring economies of scale in their manufacture. The company also marketed formulations, but that division languished till almost the early 1990s. The focus has now shifted to marketing of formulations.

DRL has been identified as a place where pharmacists and pharmacy chemists learn and develop their careers. While many of them join and work with DRL for many years before going abroad for their higher studies, for a long time DRL suffered from a phenomenon common to the Indian pharma industry. Numerous small bulk-drugs manufacturers mushrooming around Hyderabad would poach on their technical professionals. However, Anji Reddy teaches us the single most important lesson about the need to possess confidence in one's technical abilities, searching for opportunities where the abilities are useful and systematically exploiting them.

Orchid Chemicals and Pharmaceuticals Ltd

(Case prepared by S.J. Phansalkar)
(Established 1993, Turnover (1997) Rs 192 crore)

K. Raghavendra Rao came from a humble background. After his hard-won MBA from IIMA, he worked in the costing departments of three companies before joining Standard Organics in Hyderabad. From there, he migrated to the Gulf, where he worked hard and was successful. He worked as the business manager of a company that first set up a hotel, then a steel mill and finally a bulk-drugs manufacturing plant. He then decided to come back and become an entrepreneur. Among the assignments he had done in the Gulf was the establishment and running of a drugs unit during which time he had built a team. All the members of this team joined him in 1993 in establishing Orchid, a 100 per cent EOU. One of the team members was a seasoned technical hand capable of setting up a factory and running bulk-drugs production units.

The drug the team chose was cephalosporin. Cephalosporins were then, as now, antibiotics which had gone out of patents protection but had not run out of their potential as

Profit & Loss Account of Dr Reddy's Laboratories

Rs lakh

	1996–97	1995–96	1994–95	1993–94	1992–93
Income					
Sales	24,993.6	22,033.1	19,757.8	17,472.4	13,333.9
Non-mfr. Income	238.7	1447.3	714.5	133.9	51.7
Total Income	25,232.3	23,480.4	20,472.3	17,606.3	13,385.6
Expenses					
Raw Materials	12,573.7	9,249.1	7,919.9	8,475.9	6,610.8
Manufacturing Exp.	1,474.7	1,093.7	872.4	653.6	591.7
Admin & Selling Exp.	1,597.5	1,258.1	915.5	743.9	504.6
Depreciation	4,655.9	5,917.5	6,019.7	3,860.8	2,480.6
Interest	579.7	384.6	336.7	198.1	259.4
Total Expenses	848.1	559.6	307.5	538.3	485.3
	21,729.6	18,462.6	16,371.7	14,470.6	10,932.4
PBT	3,502.7	5,017.8	4,100.6	3,135.7	2,453.2
Tax	150.0	0.00	100.0	615.0	400.0
PAT	3,352.7	5,017.8	4,000.6	2,520.7	2,053.2

Source: Annual Reports

Balance Sheet of Dr Reddy's Laboratories as on 31 March

Rs lakh

	1997	1996	1995	1994	1993
Sources of Funds					
Shareholders' Funds					
Share Capital	2,648.7	2,648.7	2,491.2	655.8	655.8
Reserves & Surplus	27,427.7	26,737.8	21,960.8	5,234.0	2,910.0
Total Shareholders' Funds	30,076.4	29,386.5	24,452.0	5,889.8	3,565.8
Loan Funds					
Secured Loan	5,185.8	2,718.2	982.6	2,289.9	3,178.0
Unsecured Loan	1,072.8	0.00	3.9	1.0	1.7
Deferred Liability	0.00	0.00	0.00	0.00	8.4
Total Loan Funds	6,258.6	2,718.2	986.5	2,290.9	3,188.1
Total Sources of Funds	36,335.0	32,104.7	25,438.5	8,180.7	6,753.9
Application of Funds					
Gross Fixed Assets	10,915.8	9,156.8	6,648.3	4,242.1	3,376.8
Less: Depreciation	2,145.7	2,137.3	1,754.8	1,019.9	821.8
Net Block	8,770.1	7,019.5	4,893.5	3,222.2	2,555.0
Capital WIP	1,273.6	810.3	498.4	255.5	220.2

(continued)

(continued)

	1997	1996	1995	1994	1993
Net Fixed Assets	10,043.7	7,829.8	5,391.9	3,477.7	2,775.2
Investments	7,678.7	7,975.5	10,253.7	13.8	1.8
Current Assets					
Debtors	10,466.7	8,797.9	6,405.6	3,403.8	1,263.1
Inventories	6,151.1	5,499.2	4,466.4	3,469.6	4,744.7
Cash & Bank	393.8	530.6	493.9	273.9	172.4
Others	12.1	200.4	72.1	0.00	0.00
Loans & Advances	3,211.8	3,063.6	1,343.9	439.8	729.5
Gross Current Assets	20,235.5	18,091.7	12,781.9	7,587.1	6,909.7
Current Liabilities	4,367.6	4,016.2	3,644.0	2,897.9	2,932.8
Net Current Assets	15,867.9	14,075.5	9,137.9	4,689.2	3,976.9
Misc. Expenses	2,744.7	2,223.9	655.0	0.00	0.00
Total Application of Funds	36,335.0	32,104.7	25,438.5	8,180.7	6,753.9

Source: Annual Reports

reliable and acceptable curative drugs. Rao also had some prior experience with that drug group. Rao put all his savings, some Rs 22 million, into the venture. Other team members also took a stake according to their abilities. They all worked through 1993 to set up a first-rate factory some 50 kilometres north of Chennai. None took salaries till the production started. Rao initially sold into mainland China, but through Hongkong traders. Consistently improving on quality and also working on developing clientele, Orchid soon started doing direct sales in three continents. The company took exceptional care in maintaining product quality in terms of purity as well as physical characteristics needed by formulators, so much so that it more or less defines the international cephalosporin standards today. Rao's second emphasis was on constant upgradation of production facilities, which now match the best in the world. The third focus was to ward off the threat of closure on pollution grounds by taking consistent and serious steps for effluent control. Orchid's is a zero-effluent factory, having installed the most exotic ETP one can find. It recycles all input water. As it expands its facilities, it will more than reap the investments made in effluent treatment by way of non-stop production, reduction in solvent usage and savings on water transport.

Rao had put all his savings in starting the unit; he raised more through an IPO. Orchid started the business with an equity of Rs 60 million and a loan of Rs 58 million. Subsequent expansions were accomplished by reinvestment of surpluses, raising extra equity and increasing debts. On the product front, Orchid has focused solely on cephalosporin and gone in for backward integration for cost savings. He established an R&D unit which has now started undertaking fundamental as well as product research. The company plans to start marketing some highly specialised formulations in the country as well as abroad. Orchid has managed its money carefully. Its export reliance is high and it is tempting for the company to speculate in the forex markets. While

Balance Sheet of Orchid as on 31 March

Rs lakh

	1994	1995	1996	1997
Source of Funds				
Shareholders' Funds				
Share Capital	600.00	867.30	1734.60	1734.60
Share Appl. Money Incl. Pre. Pending Alloc.		3469.20		
Reserves & Surpluses	70.33	3600.48	7517.34	9818.75
Loan Funds				
Secured Loan	1185.03	2803.40	3498.77	6928.30
Unsecured Loan	50.00			
Hire Purchase Finance			2056.95	844.16
Total	1905.36	10740.38	14807.66	19325.81
Application of Funds				
Fixed Assets				
Gross Block	1150.84	2699.48	10307.68	13695.66
Less: Depreciation	16.17	110.10	386.99	1012.36
Net Block	1134.66	2589.38	9920.69	12683.30
Capital WIP	37.57	988.25	499.11	1206.46
Advance for Capital Items	33.65	237.51	542.88	672.07

Pre-operative Expenses Pending Allocation	1205.89	3815.14	10962.68	14561.83
Investments	1.16	133.07	1.57	51.90
	0.50	646.19	389.84	19.90
Current Assets Loans and Advances				
Interest Accrued on Investments	0.01	0.02	0.02	0.02
Inventories	305.66	878.27	3041.12	3779.08
Sundry Debtors	496.59	1872.06	80.23	1163.00
Cash and Bank Balances	156.33	2458.09	1059.99	2526.27
Other Current Assets	16.86	51.98	32.93	20.55
Loans and Advances	58.42	2538.70	1717.33	1096.57
	1033.86	7799.11	5931.62	8585.49
Less: Current Liabilities and Provisions	409.74	1761.47	3330.89	4001.07
	624.12	6037.64	2600.73	4584.42
Miscellaneous Expenditure				
Preliminary Exp.	1.97	1.77	1.57	1.37
Share Issue Exp.	52.70	89.49	105.95	93.17
Trial Production Exp.	19.03	17.10	15.16	13.22
	73.69	108.35	122.68	107.76
Total	1905.36	10740.38	14077.50	19325.81

Source: Annual Reports

numerous forex pundits crowd Orchid for attention to assist it in this regard, the company seldom goes beyond minimal hedging to protect its manufacturing earnings.

Orchid shares some of the attributes of the new-generation successful corporates: peopled by smiling and radiant youth furiously clicking onto computers in spick and span workplaces, working in an informal yet purposive manner. Decision making in Orchid has a strong group focus. Youngsters are encouraged to take up evening courses and advance their careers. Orchid pays for such course work. All appear to share Rao's vision of becoming the biggest name in the world cephalosporins market.

Biocon India Ltd

(Case prepared by S.J. Phansalkar)
(Established 1978, Turnover (1997) Rs 50 crore)

Padmashri Kiran Muzumdar started her unusual career by studying to become a brew master. That profession was hitherto regarded as an exclusive preserve of men. An Irishman approached her to start a business of producing fish moss (isinglass) and she went ahead. While she experienced wonderful cooperation from the licensing and other authorities, she soon discovered that restricting herself just to production of isinglass would mean drab, uninspiring and perhaps ill-paying business. She started acquiring knowledge and expertise in fermentation technology. Her interest was not in antibiotics but in enzymes, the metabolites of microorganisms produced during fermentation. With a team of highly qualified and motivated young scientists, she went on to establish a speciality business of manufacturing enzymes for diverse applications. The technical team created a unique system of integrating product development, marketing and applications assistance to buyers of the enzymes. The result

Profit & Loss Account of Orchid

Rs lakh

	1994	1995	1996	1997
Income				
Sales	505.50	4357.05	11188.43	19252.68
Other Op. Inc.	28.62	288.04	28.25	115.49
Misc. Income			298.87	105.14
WIP & FG	78.11	63.40	153.26	411.42
	612.24	4708.49	11668.81	19884.73
Expenditure				
RM Consumed	446.82	3179.11	7657.74	11296.73
Mfg, Selling & Other Exp.	48.61	569.42	1267.61	3188.22
Interest & Finance Chrgs	34.43	270.24	716.72	1564.66
Depreciation	10.80	94.33	276.89	717.29
Miscellaneous Exp. W/O	1.25	12.18	13.09	14.92
	541.91	4125.28	9932.05	16781.82

(continued)

(continued)

	1994	*1995*	*1996*	*1997*
Profit				
PBT	70.33	583.21	1736.76	3102.91
Less Provision for Tax	0.00	0.00	0.00	38.28
PAT	70.33	583.21	1736.76	3064.63
Balance B/f		70.33	404.58	719.54
Bal Available for Appropriation	70.33	653.53	2141.34	3784.17
Appropriation				
Trsf. to Gen Reserve		100.00	1000.00	2000.00
Proposed Dividend		148.95	421.80	693.84
Tax on Distributed Profit				69.38
Balance Carried to B/S	70.33	404.58	719.54	1020.95

Source: Annual Reports

was a successful and obviously highly profitable business. Biocon avoided becoming another antibiotic manufacturer since it did not want to become a commodity producer. The Biocon group has four companies sharing common facilities and services: a 100 per cent EOU, a company half-owned by Unilever, a pure contract research company and now a commercial manufacturer of speciality bio-drugs.

Aside from commercial activities, Biocon maintains a highly proactive scientific interest. It has built a biodiversity programme of its own. On its own initiative, it is building up a bank (germplasm) of tropical micro-organisms. They propose to research the metabolites of these micro-organisms. It is possible that some of the metabolites may become commercially useful.

Consistent with the demands of the business, the Biocon group hires exceptionally well-qualified people, often fresh from college, then trains them and retains them by the sheer freedom to grow professionally. They have above average salaries, an elegant and refined work environment and the constant company of professionals. The group is innovating in the field of employee rewards by way of employees' stock option plans, not only for the directors and all technical people, who have already been so rewarded, but also for staff at various levels.

Biocon started with a loan from the Karnataka State Financial Corporation (KSFC), established the second unit through TDICI finances and has now graduated to ICICI financing.

An indicative statement about the Financial Implications of Operations of Biocon (figures as per cent of sales) is given below:

Sales	100
Inputs (Covering Materials, Fuel, Power and Direct Labour)	55
Salaries & Benefits	5
Admin. Overheads	15
Including Interest	5
R&D	4

(continued)

(continued)

Depreciation	2
Profit	25
Tax	10
PAT	15

Mastek Limited

(Case prepared by S.J. Phansalkar and Shyamal Gupta)
(Established 1982, Turnover (1997) Rs 71 crore)

Four classmates of IIMA 1979 PGP batch, Ashank Desai, R. Sundar, Vasan and Ketan Mehta, decided during the course of their second year at IIMA that they would set up their own enterprise connected with software. Coming from middle-class families, each had to work for a few years before putting their ideas into practice. Starting a management and software consulting firm in 1982, they chose applications software as their main line.

As the computer acceptance, use, configurations and status of software underwent changes in the past few years, Mastek kept pace and at times managed to ride the crest of these changes. They began by developing specific tailor-made applications software on mainframes or such systems as were owned by their clients. They were the first to have introduced domestically developed canned software products (an accounting software package and a package for stockbrokers). They set up their branch network in the country to market these packages. By 1990, relational data base management system (RDBMS) had become acceptable to large Indian businesses. Mastek became the early marketers of (RDBMS) and grew rapidly as an organisation engaged in programmes and applications consulting on Ingress systems.

By the early 1990s, they started moving abroad. They set up shop first in Singapore and then in the US. Sundar migrated to the US, looking after their US interests. Their chosen mode was to set up subsidiary companies with their own staff in the host countries, rather than servicing the clients from India. Today they have subsidiaries in four countries, headed by a local person and operating as autonomous profit centres. With the onset of the body-shopping dominated software exports business, they have fallen slightly behind.

Mastek hired professionals first from the IITs and IIMs. Their young recruits enjoyed working with people not much older than themselves and having similar professional attitudes and outlook. Ashank was very particular and meticulous about recruitment procedures and never compromised on standards. Insider recommendations were sure black hats for the recruit. As these whiz-kids started becoming increasingly eager to fly West, Mastek had to change their recruitment focus to ensure stability in the workforce. They started focusing mainly on regional engineering colleges. Retention of young software professionals is a problem with which they need to grapple like everyone else in the industry.

Mastek's success lay in that they identified the right opportunity and stuck with the line. Despite having four high-flying MBAs at the helm of affairs, they avoided getting into management consulting as they thought it was too general a line. They supplemented their software applications activity with R&D effort for which they established a Product Development Centre. Mastek financed their business through internal accruals for the first eight years. They took a TDICI loan for the Product Development Centre and also made an IPO in 1993. Mastek have resisted the temptation to be incorporated into cash rich corporates. They have also stayed away from shifting to alternate product or business lines, including computer training. Simplicity, informality and frugality characterised their initial business. Even as a relatively larger company, they installed office equipment at their corporate office as elsewhere only in phases. 'Lean and mean' is their motto. Part of the reason for the sustained frugality in Indian operations was the fact that their subsidiaries abroad are not capitalised on scales so as to be able to obtain loans in the host country and hence Mastek has to service their working capital needs. Mastek moved from a system of 'pooled' software resources shared by several subsidiaries to one of 'overseas factories' of these subsidiaries in India. The heads of these factories report to their bosses abroad for whom they exclusively work.

Professional recognition followed as Ashank became the Chairman of the NASSCOM in the mid-1990s. The initial group stuck together without personality clashes since they consistently followed a team approach. Looking at Mastek, one observer said, 'This company demonstrates, if any thing, the fact that we have moved from the era of individual entrepreneurship to one of group entrepreneurship.'

Profit & Loss Statement of Mastek

Rs lakh

	30 Jun. 94	30 Jun. 95	30 Jun. 96
Income	1,977.94	2,210.62	2,934.87
Expenditure			
Expenses	1,392.77	1514.17	2024.63
Depreciation	84.88	152.02	234.88
Interest & Finance Charges	78.80	112.91	246.25
	1,556.45	1,779.10	2,505.76
Profit Before Tax	421.49	431.52	429.11
Less: Provision for Tax	34.20	10.00	15.00
Profit After Tax	387.29	421.52	414.11
Add Bal B/f	52.34	59.65	75.87
Bal Available for Appropriation	439.63	481.17	489.98
Appropriation			
Dividend Subject to Ded. of Tax	104.98	105.30	109.93
Transferred to Gen. Reserves	275.00	300.00	300.00
Balance Carried to B/S	59.65	75.87	80.05
	439.63	481.17	489.98

Source: Annual Reports

Balance Sheet of Mastek

Rs lakh

	30 Jun. 94	30 Jun. 95	30 Jun. 96
Source of Funds			
Shareholders' Funds			
Share Capital	299.94	305.62	344.41
Reserves & Surpluses	927.22	1249.22	2251.54
Loan Funds			
Secured Loan	225.70	650.76	703.22
Unsecured Loan	62.21	115.00	100.00
Total	1515.07	2320.60	3399.17
Application of Funds			
Fixed Assets			
Gross Block	526.36	1071.19	1603.02
Less: Depreciation	148.95	300.98	535.86
Net Block	377.41	770.21	1067.16
Capital WIP	149.39	221.18	128.22
	526.80	991.39	1195.38
Investments	154.52	309.23	473.50
Current Assets Loans and Advances			
Sundry Debtors	590.46	1025.89	1690.43
Cash and Bank Balances	583.21	335.63	200.19
Loans & Advances	146.63	338.89	385.74
Less: Current Liabilities and Provisions			
Liabilities	388.43	584.34	486.78
Provisions	134.01	127.35	134.93
Net Current Assets	797.86	988.72	1654.65
Miscellaneous Expenditure	35.89	31.26	75.64
Total	1515.07	2320.60	3399.17

Source: Annual Reports

Sumangal Press (P) Limited (*Kalnirnaya*)

(Case prepared by Ajit Kanitkar)
(Established 1973, Turnover (1997) Rs 20 crore)

Jayant Salgaonkar wrote the crossword puzzle and the astrology columns for *Loksatta*, a popular Marathi daily, for years before quitting the job and starting on his own. He simplified the traditional almanac (*panchang*), organised it in the form of a calendar and his product was born! The product, first launched in Marathi in 1973, was called '*Kalnirnaya*' (the verdict of time). Till that time, virtually no one ever purchased a calendar. Calendars were then, as now, viewed as promotion material of commercial organisations. Almost every company worth its name printed and distributed calendars. As did the local traders, merchants and others. Thus most homes got calendars as free gifts.

In such a situation, Salgaonkar found it difficult to even get a distributor. But they were proved wrong. In 1973, the first print order of 5,000 copies proved too small and two more print runs had to be taken. The next year, the volume rose to 25,000 copies. It has been climbing up ever since. Salgaonkar started marketing the space on calendars for commercial advertisers. He innovated on using the reverse sides of the calendar pages for printing articles of general interest written by eminent and popular writers. Buying *Kalnirnaya* around November–December has become a ritual. It has become a symbol of Maharashtrian culture. Sumangal's TV jingle '*bhintivari kalnirnaya asawe*' (the last line of a jingle that describes a complete Marathi household, it means that the wall is adorned with *Kalnirnaya*) became immensely popular and was no exaggeration.

Editions in different languages and focusing on different issues started. In 1997, the volume reached over five million copies. The initial distributors were booksellers and this set has been expanded to include the company's own distribution network at the district level, feeding semi-wholesellers and eventually the bookstall owners or pedestrian vendors.

To begin with, Salgaonkar printed the calendar on job-work basis. The 1979 elections put him in great trouble as the government had blocked all printing capacity for printing of ballots. That taught him a lesson. To support the printing load, Salgaonkar established his own printing presses, first at Andheri and then at Thane. These were expanded and modernised in due course of time, and are managed by a division called Sumangal Artech. The division focuses on printing *Kalnirnaya* during August–October (new year's calendars start appearing by November) and markets the printing facility the rest of the year.

Salgaonkar's three sons have joined him in the business. The eldest, who studied economics, is the MD. The second, an engineer, supervises the printing facilities. The youngest, an architect, manages the artwork and designing. They hold together simply because they have been through some very tough periods when the enterprise was a fledgling. And they realise that together they do much better.

Salgaonkar has reached a sales volume of over Rs 200 million and has been profitable in most of his ventures, except when he started a newspaper called *Kalnirnaya Vartaman*. Recently, *Kalnirnaya* went electronic and established a website offering commercial information on Indian companies. Salgaonkar has also started publishing databooks on the line of the Tatas. The USP is that chronologically it comes out the first. Salgaonkar always stays ahead of time so that the *kalnirnaya* (verdict of time) will be favourable to him.

Praj Industries Limited

(Case prepared by Ajit Kanitkar)
(Established 1985, Turnover (1997) Rs 60 crore)

Pramod Chowdhari, an engineer who worked with Widia India and later with Rapicut, started a line somewhat unrelated to his experience. He went through a very thorough process of identifying suitable lines of business. His father's rapport with the sugar cooperatives and the potential opportunity in the line prompted him to get into distillery project design, erection and commissioning. Rather than just restricting to technical design and engineering, Praj began a new style of functioning of offering a complete range of services including project report preparation, assistance in seeking concessional as well as bank finance, steering the proposal through various stages of clearances pertaining to distillery line, and so on.

Chowdhari identified a gap in ethanol production technology. The equipment used in the country used conventional batch-type fermentation process. Alpha Laval Limited, the only supplier of continuous fermentation-type equipment, started doing this business around the same time. Chowdhari tied up with an Austrian firm from whom Praj obtained the technology. The actual fabrication of equipment was done initially in third-party job shops. Praj also spent time and developed a distillery effluents treatment plant branded Spranhilator. His next move was to tie up with companies abroad for brewery engineering technology and for manufacture of plate heat exchangers, which could be used in dairy machinery or other processes. By the mid-1990s, Praj shifted attention towards distillery equipment which could handle materials other than molasses. Finally they diversified into pharmaceutical process engineering and plant manufacture.

The outsourced manufacturing system was replaced first by own factories, scattered in several locations, and later merged into a centralised facility for designing and detailed engineering of equipment to be installed. Keeping in mind the future needs of the processing industry in the country, the company has identified four areas for itself: plant and equipments for bio-commodities processing and effluent treatment; plant and equipment for food and pharma sectors in the country; separation systems for drying, dewatering, concentration, etc; and heat transfer equipment such as heat exchangers. The company also focuses on integrated systems and modules using one or more of the above. Praj has gone international by setting up a company in Singapore.

As an exclusively project erection company, their asset base had been low in the initial stages and they relied upon customer advances as the main source of finance for their operations. The first term loan was taken from SBI Home Finance for the construction of their integrated engineering and marketing facilities and offices. TDICI finance and an IPO followed in 1994. The long-term financial needs are met today mainly by own funds. The dominant use of resources is in financing current assets. Praj thus shifted from engineering services (along with additional services for single-window assistance in project clearance) and strengths to core engineering competencies, from a highly restricted set of distillery-related activity to a more broadbased set of business profile and geographical expansion, all in a span of 10 years. All the while, financing was conservative.

Profit & Loss Account of Praj Industries

Rs lakh

	1992	1993	1994	1995	1996
Sales	1607	3178	3755	5995	5579
Other Income	012	48	68	175	78
Manufacturing Exp.	1555	2396	2762	4420	3858
Personnel Exp.—Incd. in Mfg. Exp.		145	204	301	408
Other Expenses—Incd. in Mfg. Exp.		348	442	716	753
Financial and Interest Charges	12	28	43	99	204
Depreciation	6	10	14	25	82
PBT	46	297	357	608	350
PAT	27	212	252	447	328

Source: Annual Reports

V-Guard Industries Ltd

(Case prepared by Vivekananda Shenoy, P.T. Pradeep and Sheela Anna Thomas)
(Established 1977, Turnover (1997) Rs 60 crore)

Kochouseph Chittilappilly comes from a family of agriculturists. After finishing his Masters he joined a PSU engaged in manufacture of electrical and electronic gadgets. He stayed with his family, and their friends often brought electronic gadgets for repairs to him. His experience in fixing them as well as his exposure in the PSU gave him the confidence to work on his own. At the end of a forced unemployment period, he asked for and surprisingly got his father's approval for starting his own business. He started making voltage stabilisers.

While he had problems having his loan sanctioned even under the young entrepreneurs' programme of nationalised banks, his father gave him money whenever asked. He started from a hired space of 450 sq. ft in Kochi. In 1977, he made 25 stabilisers for refrigerators and tried to sell them through distributors. His personal contacts helped him get his products displayed in elite shops in Ernakulam. He priced the stabilisers at Rs 10 more than the leading brands, on the premise that his product offered additional features.

Soon he started selling upwards of 50 stabilisers a month and in a year, the sales were over 200 pieces per month. He expanded the product line to cover stabilisers, deep fridges and television sets. He manufactured the pieces at several locations, using different names for each location but a common brand name. The sales rose rapidly and he crossed a turnover of a crore by 1984. This style of manufacturing caused him severe problems when in 1986, there was a raid by the Central Excise Department who imposed a demand of Rs 46 lakh on him. He discovered that inadequate care in maintaining accounts and keeping documents at various locations was a greater disadvantage in fighting the ensuing litigation. He then became very careful and meticulous in proper accounts keeping, hiring staff and professional chartered accountants. Labour unrest in his manufacturing facilities despite what he considered liberal payment policies made him think of options to factory-centred manufacture. He experimented with charitable organisations which were too happy to have the products assembled in their premises as income-generating activities for their inmates. V-Guard found the experiment successful as they deployed their own quality assurance personnel at each location and did not compromise on quality. In a year or so, he closed his own manufacturing units after retrenching the employees and developed systems that enabled him to continue operations at full scale relying entirely on such outside arrangements. But for a strong brand backed by widely recognised high product quality, the company would have found it difficult to maintain high volumes in a competitive market. While the company has high sales (Rs 60 crore), its assets base is small. Consequently, their ability to borrow in formal channels is limited. Working capital needs force them to borrow at relatively high interest rates from friends and relatives. Gradually changing the relationship between V-Guard and the distributors from principal–agent to seller–buyer, with appropriate adjustment in margins to take care of sales tax complications, is expected to reduce the inventory costs and hence working capital need.

Ashima Syntex Limited

(Case prepared by Shyamal Gupta)
(Established 1982, Turnover (1997) Rs 212 crore)

Chintan Parikh came from a business family. While studying for a Fellow programme in management at IIMA, he decided to go into his business. He started two small companies prior to joining hands with Sanjay Lalbhai in floating

Ashima. Then Chintan played around, setting up several businesses as diverse as metals and melmoware. This was done as he felt that becoming large in any one single line was more a liability than a smart move. One of the companies floated was Anagram Finance, also in partnership with Lalbhai. Only after 1992 did he settle down to one business, relinquishing his stake in Anagram in favour of Lalbhai and gaining their stake in Ashima.

Ashima was a small polyester texturising unit, a line which was actively being promoted by Reliance for marketing their output. The field became quite crowded. Ashima first expanded capacity several times in the same line, but then had to decide to carve out a field for itself and move out of the shadow of both the Lalbhais and Reliance.

Ashima focused on denim manufacture. It also acquired sick textile mills contagious to its factory locations and created a fully integrated textile-processing complex, the largest integrated complex in the country's textile industry. Divisions manufacturing denim cloth, value-added cotton fabrics, knitted fabrics, ready-to-stitch and ready-to-wear lines were added between 1992 and 1997.

These expansions needed money. The funds were obtained by way of IPO of convertible debentures in 1993, rights issues of shares in 1994 and private placement of shares at a large premium in 1995. The company has a large portfolio of projects which it actively seeks to implement in future.

Extraordinary operational freedom given to young professionals hired to manage the company and strong focus on HRD make it a good company to work with from the point of view of the employees. IBM recognised it as one of their best clients in the world—something which demonstrates their commitment to thrive in the new IT world.

Systematic exploitation of one closely related product line after 1992 and efforts to develop a competitive edge in processing efficiency established the company on sound footing. Of late, the attention on marketing and brand creation is

Profit & Loss Account of Ashima Syntex

Rs lakh

	Jun. 97	Jun. 96	Jun. 95	Jun. 94
Income				
Sales of Goods & Services	21,291.88	15,816.73	8,286.78	3,726.49
Business Income			77.98	200.76
Other Income	842.93	371.44	722.22	404.04
Increase in Stock			2,280.79	70.86
Total (I)	22,134.81	16,188.17	11,367.77	4,402.15
Expenditure				
Manufacturing and Other Expenses	17,725.35	10,533.33	8,421.27	2,969.34
Employees Emoluments	868.43	418.89	205.51	80.45
Administrative and Other Expenses	1,027.63	590.99	366.60	235.99
Interest & Finance Charges	571.31	135.22	240.85	330.22
Depreciation	1,321.30	826.41	539.10	177.49
Amortization of Expenses	139.51	61.32	29.58	10.21
(Increase)/Decrease in Stock	(2,546.31)	1,494.91		
Total (II)	19,107.22	14,061.07	9,802.91	3,803.70

(continued)

(continued)

	Jun. 97	Jun. 96	Jun. 95	Jun. 94
Previous Years Adjustment			1.21	3.71
Profit Before Tax	3,027.59	2,127.10	1,566.07	602.16
Provision for Tax Including Wealth Tax	371.00	0.31		64.00
Profit After Tax	2,656.59	2,126.79	1,566.07	538.16
Prior Period Adjustment	2.98	(1.43)		
Balance b/f From Previous Year	2,659.57	2,125.36	1,566.07	538.16
	2,206.43	1,282.33	558.49	299.97
Balance Available for Appropriation	4,866.00	3,407.69	2,124.56	838.13
Appropriations				
Trans. to Debenture Redemption Reserve	633.40	396.23	266.68	85.52
Trans. to General Reserve	270.00	220.00	160.00	70.00
Proposed Dividend	870.40	584.73	415.55	124.12
Tax on Dividend	87.04		NA	NA
Balance Carried to Balance Sheet	3,005.16	2,206.43	1,282.33	558.49
	4,866.00	3,407.39	2,124.56	838.13

Source: Annual Reports

Balance Sheet of Ashima Syntex Ltd

Rs lakh

	Jun. 97	Jun. 96	Jun. 95	Jun. 94
Sources of Funds				
Shareholders' Fund				
Share Capital	3,335.03	2,627.66	1,860.60	544.24
Share Application Money	0.00	450.00	0.00	0.00
Reserves & Surplus	17,738.64	12,662.90	7,338.01	1,480.39
	21,073.67	15,740.56	9,198.61	2,024.63
Loan Funds				
Secured Loan				
Debentures	4,900.00	2,000.00	2,000.00	2,500.00
Debentures Application Money	0.00	2,700.00	0.00	0.00
Term Loan and Working Capital Facilities	6,857.23	7,056.40	4,471.46	1,140.20
Short-term Loans for New Projects	993.75	688.75	3,452.67	2,277.53
	12,750.98	12,445.15	9,924.13	5,917.73
Unsecured Loan	3,944.33	3,549.83	1,450.26	671.70
	16,695.31	15,994.98	11,374.39	6,589.43
Total	37,768.98	31,735.54	20,573.00	8,614.06

(continued)

(continued)

Rs lakh

	Jun. 97	Jun. 96	Jun. 95	Jun. 94
Application of Funds				
Fixed Assets				
Gross Block	21,803.57	13,075.30	10,093.01	2,814.52
Less: Depreciation fund	2,883.29	1,800.84	985.13	446.30
Net Block	18,920.28	11,274.46	9,107.88	2,368.22
Capital WIP	2,390.55	6,538.12	1,911.38	1,536.45
Investment	4,999.12	3,679.77	2,038.59	1,657.04
Current Assets, Loans and Advances				
Inventories	6,463.66	3,515.63	3,787.67	544.65
Sundry Debtors	3,082.14	2,674.08	2,002.38	1,435.91
Cash and Bank Balances	1,199.16	2,692.56	809.23	662.81
Other Current Assets	530.44	567.92	563.24	335.66
Loans & Advances	4,314.61	3,513.63	2,443.59	930.73
	15,590.01	12,963.82	9,606.11	3,909.76
Current Liabilities and Provisions				
Liabilities	3,170.37	2,286.80	1,762.29	629.96
Provisions	1,388.76	638.58	467.36	251.51
	4,559.13	2,925.38	2,229.65	881.47
Net Current Assets	11,030.88	10,038.44	7,376.46	3,028.29
Miscellaneous Expenditure	428.15	204.75	138.69	24.06
Total	37,768.98	31,735.54	20,573.00	8,614.06

Source: Annual Reports

giving it a new push. All in all, the company will give a good run for its money to Arvind.

Sudha Agro-Oils and Chemical Industries Ltd

(Case prepared by S.J. Phansalkar)
(Established 1981, Turnover (1997) Rs 55 crore)

E. Raja Rao belongs to an agricultural family of West Godavari district. After doing his B.A. in economics, he worked in three companies. Around 1974, when that part of the country took to rice bran (RB) processing in a big way, he set up a rice bran-processing factory with some of his friends. By 1982, he left that group and set up Sudha Agro-Oils and Chemical Industries Ltd in Samalkot. Initially he had only a 150 tonnes per day (TDP) solvent extraction plant.

Rice bran oil (RBO) produced by him is mainly sold to HLL, Tata, and Godrej. De-oiled rice bran extractions are exported to European countries. Raja Rao employs largely from local resources. The key functions have been handled by family members. As a first step in value addition, he added an industrial hydrogenation plant for hydrogenation of RBO. Chemical refining of RBO followed, and then physical refining. In the late 1980s when oil meal exports business became prominent, instead of entering it, Raja Rao chose to lease his processing facilities to ITC and then to Essar Gujarat, while he himself focused on expansion and diversification in his factory. A physical refining unit, expansion of the physical refining capacity, fatty acid distillation plant and oxygen recovery and bottling plants were added in quick succession between 1991 and 1996. As of now, Sudha has the most completely integrated RB processing plant in the country.

Raja Rao achieved phenomenal capacity utilisation of the solvent extraction (SE) plant but decided not to invest in expanding it as larger operations would need even greater working capital and expose him more to price volatility. Nor did he invest in promoting a consumer brand of edible RB oil. Efficient continuous processing of rice bran and its derivatives was his focus and that is where he concentrated. Retained earnings and IDBI loans financed his expansion. Equity was closely held and all temptation of IPO was resisted.

Raja Rao presents the image of a conservative, careful businessman who knows what he wants and has the patience to achieve it.

Balance Sheet of Sudha Agro-Oils and Chemicals as on 31 March

Rs lakh

	1992	1993	1994	1995	1996	1997
Liabilities						
Share Capital	53.5	53.5	123.0	178.0	178.0	225.0
Reserves & Surplus	92.3	104.0	70.9	166.0	230.0	113.0
Secured Loans	00.9	00.0	195.0	671.0	1091.0	1058.0
Unsecured Loans	41.0	48.0	49.0	56.0	87.0	112.0
Provisions	12.6	09.6	10.3	23.0	27.0	31.0
Current Liabilities	84.8	36.2	42.0	240.0	501.0	618.0
Total	285.1	251.3	490.2	1334.0	2114.0	2157.0
Assets						
Gross Block	273.0	278.0	405.0	944.0	1181.0	1191.0
Less: Depreciation	132.0	151.0	163.0	196.0	243.0	427.0
Net Block	141.0	127.0	242.0	748.0	938.0	764.0
CWIP	00.0	00.0	27.0	00.0	01.0	05.0
Investments	00.0	00.0	01.0	01.0	01.0	01.0
Inventories	113.0	21.0	40.0	420.0	823.0	843.0
Sundry Debtors	49.2	39.4	24.0	108.0	264.0	456.0
Advances	51.3	39.9	206.0	05.1	57.6	62.0
Cash and Bank	07.0	13.0	08.0	09.0	21.0	12.0
Other Current Assets	14.4	11.0	09.0	02.0	06.0	12.0
Total	285.1	251.3	490.2	1334.0	2114.0	2157.0

Source: Annual Reports

Profit & Loss Account of Sudha Agro-Oils and Chemicals Ltd

Rs lakh

	1992	1993	1994	1995	1996	1997
Sales	927.0	575.0	103.0	2310.0	3178.0	3968.0
Processing Charges	191.0	238.0	280.0	156.0	133.0	69.0
Other Income	05.0	09.0	04.0	09.0	33.0	46.0
Cost of Goods Sold						
Raw Material	685.0	442.0	91.0	1881.0	2455.0	2878.0
Processing Charges	93.0	52.0	00.0	00.0	00.0	00.0
Power & Fuel	75.3	84.3	111.0	134.0	215.0	293.0
Pkg. Chemicals & Stores	52.0	60.0	61.0	104.0	144.0	210.0
Repairs & Maintenance	31.0	13.0	22.0	20.0	36.0	42.0
Misc Mfg. Exp.	11.0	13.0	12.0	15.0	31.0	42.0
Wages / Salaries & Other Benefits	17.0	17.0	18.0	27.0	54.0	79.0
Selling Exp.	63.0	45.0	03.0	36.0	80.0	169.0
Admin Exp.	17.0	18.0	16.0	25.0	31.5	36.0
Taxes & Rates	30.0	13.0	03.0	20.0	47.0	64.0
Interest	11.0	15.0	09.0	77.0	143.0	202.0
Depreciation	20.0	20.0	13.0	32.0	47.0	197.0
Net Profit	17.0	27.0	26.0	102.0	82.0	-92.0
Income Tax	01.0	04.0	06.0	11.0	00.0	00.0
PAT	16.0	23.0	19.4	91.0	82.0	-92.0

Source: Annual Reports

3

Learning from Success: An Illustration of a Case and its Analysis

This book is written informally. Statements made in later chapters about specific decisions taken by companies will appear simple and direct, while the logic for them may not appear explicit. The reader may then feel that I am indulging in *obiter dicta*. While he may still feel the same after reading this chapter, the intention is to offer an illustration of a case and its analysis. Most of the statements in the book are based on similar analysis. A friend who read the pre-publication draft felt that only on reading one full case does much of what I write fall in place. Those who wish to know the logic behind the statements are welcome to read this chapter. Others may read it as a mere story full of industrial human interest. The case of Sun Pharmaceutical Industries Limited and my observations thereon will facilitate an understanding of the nature of the process of drawing inferences.

Sun Pharmaceutical Industries Limited

Dilip Shanghvi, Managing Director of the Sun Pharmaceutical Industries Limited, Vadodara, is credited with pioneering the spectacular growth of his company. Starting on third-party manufacture basis in Calcutta in the late 1978, Sun moved westwards in 1982. From a manufacturing facility in Vapi costing Rs 1 million in 1982, the company in 1997 has four own factories and has acquired control in two pharmaceutical units in Gujarat. It has reached a turnover of Rs 160 crore in 1997 and its market capitalisation exceeds Rs 300 crore. This case attempts to describe the evolution of Sun.

A Brief History

Dilip Shanghvi studied commerce in Calcutta. During and after his college education, he spent time in the shop run by his father Shri Shantilal Shanghvi. Their firm B.N. Enterprises worked as stockists for Torrent, Tamilnadu Dadha and some other pharmaceutical companies. Dilip Shanghvi was curious about why and how some drugs rather than others move in some markets rather than others. He would talk to the salesmen and other sales people who visited the shop and exchange his ideas and analysis about these matters with them. He also developed friendship with some medical practitioners. One of them, Dr Bavishi, was to prove immensely supportive and helpful in Dilip Shanghvi's choice of products later on.

In 1978, he started marketing two formulations: Lithosun and Nitrosun, both for use in psychiatric therapy. His firm was known as Sun Pharmaceutical Industries. The formulations were produced in the factory of a third party, under loan license scheme. The Gujarati community in Bengal is fairly close-knit and owing to his father's connections in the pharma distribution line, Dilip Shanghvi was able to spread the marketing effort within Bengal. His firm continues to remain particularly strong in psychiatric therapy drugs and in East India till date.

By the early 1980s, he concluded that for a pharmaceutical company, West Bengal was not the ideal location. Products of companies located in Gujarat and Maharashtra were better accepted. Also, he felt that sound and technically competent manpower in this field was difficult to come by in West Bengal. It so happened that around that time the then Chief Minister of Gujarat visited Calcutta to woo the Gujarati community to come back and set up industries in Gujarat. By 1981, Shanghvi decided to move his base to Gujarat. He supplemented his funds by personal loans from friends and relatives, and with the help of institutional loans, established the manufacturing shed in Vapi. It was a standard 1800 sq. ft industrial shed of GIDC, to which additions were made for providing space for quality checking, quarantine storage and such special requirements of formulation units. The initial investment in plant and machinery was about Rs 7 lakh. Kamlesh Dudhara (now Vice President, Formulations Development) and Lad (now Sr Manager, Quality Control, at Silvassa) joined him for managing the production in Vapi unit. The firm continued to operate under the name of Sun Pharmaceutical Industries. His partners Nitin Mehta, Shailesh Desai and Upen Shanghvi joined him as the business took off. Dilipbhai himself focused on marketing the formulations. Nitinbhai managed the factory while Upenbhai was responsible for purchases. Sun had an office in West Vile Parle in Mumbai, in the premises owned by one of the family members. Some staff was hired for assisting in office administration, documentation, follow up, etc., but the main staff strength (10 field salespersons) was in marketing. Commercial operations were done from Mumbai. Nitinbhai as well as Dilipbhai commuted to Vapi. They sold Lithosun, Nitrosun, Trazin, Amixide and Eliwel made from Vapi. All these are used in psychiatric therapy.

Sun experienced a cash crunch in 1983, due to the investment made in the plant at Vapi. Being in a high-margin business, Sun came out of the trouble soon. Suppliers of materials gave them credit. Sun learnt an important lesson that reinforced its philosophy of opting for long-term relations with suppliers based on mutual respect and trust.

The Vapi unit had to be expanded almost within one year. This second phase of expansion (the first was done at the start itself) cost about Rs 30 lakh. All the profits were continuously ploughed back in the factory expansion. A distribution centre was acquired in Vapi in 1984 for handling dispatches. Following is an indicative funds flow statement.

Indicative Funds Flow Statement for Years 1982–85–88–90–93

Rs lakh

	1982	1985	1988	1990	1993
Sales	12	60	450	972	3138
Source of Funds					
Equity	1	1	1	1	641
Surpluses	0	16	120	279	28
Personal Loans	6	15	64	0	0
Other Unsecured Loans	4		20	100	211
F.I. Finances		14	60	300	641
Total					
Uses of Funds Net Block	7	30	150	450	639
Working Capital	4	15	115	230	882

Source: 1993 figures are actuals reported in the *Prospectus* of the company issued in 1994. Other figures are surmises based on discussions with various executives.

Scaling Up

By 1985, Sun had reached a volume of about Rs 5 lakh a month. Further growth appeared possible but creation of larger manufacturing base was needed for that. Expansion at Vapi was constrained by space. Sun would have lost the excise and related advantages available to small-scale units if the expansion was done at Vapi. Dilipbhai's family members started another firm under the name of Unimed and established a plant at Halol in Vadodara district. Simultaneously, loan license arrangements were in vogue with some other suppliers as well.

Unimed is now treated as a deemed public limited company. It has always been run by the management of Sun, but commercial transactions are kept apart. 'The decision to set up Unimed as a separate entity was made within the constraints which were imposed by regulations and in the mindset of a small-scale entrepreneur. Today I would not do such a thing!,' says Dilipbhai.

After 1985, Sun has been investing in the expansion of manufacturing facilities every year. A 'single therapy company' for several years, it introduced in 1988 two formulations, Angizem and Monotrate, for cardiovascular therapy. Several other drugs for this therapy were subsequently introduced. Sun also went national in marketing that year.

The operating organisational structure of Sun looked like this in 1988:

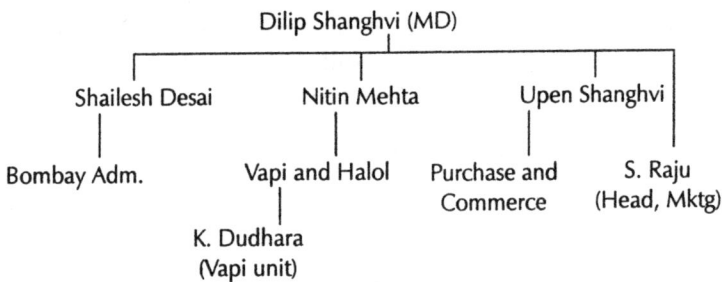

In 1989, the necessity of coordinating the Halol and Vapi units as well as several third-party loan license manufacturers led to the establishment of the corporate office at Vadodara. In that year (1988–89), Sun was ranked 107th as per the ORG

Retail Chain Audit, selling about Rs five crore worth of medicines. Its rank in psychiatric therapy was much higher. By 1990, Sun had started selling medicines worth Rs one crore a month. The next year onwards, Sun started looking seriously at export opportunities.

In 1990, all properties of Sun Pharmaceutical Industries were vested in a company called Sun Pharmaceutical Industries Limited (the present company) by operation of law. In 1992, Sun started marketing drugs for special gastro-intestinal problems. The drug Famotidine was introduced under the brand name Famocid to compete with Ranitidine (being sold under the brand name of Zinetac by Glaxo). Sun (as we shall call the going concern for its entire lifespan) set up a modern R&D centre called Sparc in Vadodara in 1993. Sun built a new formulations unit at Silvassa in 1994. Its bulk drugs unit at Panoli also went into operations from that year. This was also the year Sun went public.

Along with its associated investment companies, Sun has since bought equity stakes in M.J. Pharmaceuticals Limited and Gujarat Lyka Organics Limited, both in Gujarat, and the manufacturing facilities of Boots (India) Limited in Ahmednagar. It has recently decided to acquire Tamilnadu Dadha Pharmaceuticals Limited. As of 1997, it sells medicines in the three fields of psychotherapy, cardiovascular therapy and gastro-intestinal therapy, and in the fourth line of special drugs for application in intensive care, introduced in 1994. Sun closed its 1996 accounts with a sales turnover of Rs 159 crore. While the sales turnover was below the sales level projected in its prospectus issued in 1994, the profit and earnings per share outperformed the projections significantly. This demonstrates what the company seems to believe in. As one executive asked the case writer, 'If we can earn Rs 10 by selling medicines worth Rs 50 in a neat and compact manner and with less effort, what is the fun of running around in circles selling medicines worth Rs 100 and earning Rs eight?' Sun employs over 1,500 persons, including 650 in marketing, and the balance in factories, corporate office and Sparc.

Core Values and Beliefs

Sun believes that it is a marketing company. All other activities within the company have to be oriented to help improve its marketing performance. There is a fairly well thought out philosophy pervading through the organisation.

Initially, the impetus to growth came from the drive and energy of Dilip Shanghvi. 'I then had little money but a lot of time. So I used my time well, thinking about products and marketing strategies, reading about new developments and learning from the market about current needs and future opportunities. Now the picture is a little different. We have more money and my time is crowded. I cannot allow the developments of my company to be contingent upon one individual any more' is how he put it. Vice President—Finance, said, 'Dilipbhai believes he is the trustee of the shareholders in this company. He owns over 70 per cent of the block, but still regards transparency and propriety of managing the company as supreme values.' To give an example, the accounts executive who debited expenses pertaining to the personal travel of the chairman was explained the mistake and the entry reversed. He was told that the chairman (Dilipbhai's father) had enough personal wealth to pay for his personal travel and only his official expenses had to be debited to Sun.

Transparency is the operative word in Sun. Unlike the usual cagey manner of mid-size Indian corporates where they would not give you the time of the day if they could help it, Sun not only shares but actually publishes a breakdown of sales by product, division and therapy. It appears not in the least inhibited about discussing their cost structure, profitability or margins. 'But why should we hide these things? We do things properly and legally. We manage our business in a manner that it makes more profits without taking a single wrong or doubtful step. So why should we be afraid?' is how one executive put it.

Dilipbhai does not believe in taking wild chances or risks with his own or shareholders' money. 'Either the technology will be new or the product will be new but not both. Either we undertake developments in a new production technology for a product which has an established market, or we introduce in the market a wholly new, first-time-in-the therapy formulation, which we know can be produced well by us. We do not wish to take risks on both production and the marketing side.'

In terms of values, Sun has an environment of purposive, energetic hard work. Concern for others, a sense of fair play, willingness to undertake fairly difficult tasks and hence work hard for them, and to take responsibility for one's decisions are some of the commonly noted 'Sun values'.

Concern for employee well-being is a strong value at Sun. Darshan, a young junior executive in Sun, narrates how he owes his very life to this value. Suffering from a congenital renal problem as he was, Darshan had a kidney failure in the early 1990s. He was then a young and junior officer, and not a key individual in any sense. The company moved swiftly, putting all its goodwill in the Vadodara medical circles as well as its organisational strength behind him. A kidney transplant was arranged and Darshan is now a smiling and enthusiastic proof of Sun's people orientation. Manoharan, a chemist in the Silvasa plant, narrates a similar but much less dramatic incident about how the 'MD sahab himself took me to a reputed dermatologist of Bombay for treating some allergy-related problem to make me feel comfortable and ensure that I do not leave Sun unnecessarily'. This feeling that Sun will care for its staff is ubiquitous and contributes to a positive attitude towards the company.

Products and Markets

Sun has followed the basic approach of marketing speciality medicines. The reason is explained by Roy, now

GM in the Synergy Division, 'An average pharma company making routine sort of medicines (OTC drugs, broad-spectrum antibiotics, analgesics and anti-pyretics, etc.) has to reach out to a large number of customers to make its sales. The salesmen meet practically every general physician. And then there is nothing so great about the usual products compared with those of the competitor, so there is very expensive promotion to be done. But how many psychiatrists and neurophysicians do you have, say, in Nagpur? Or cardiac specialists for that matter? If you focus on speciality medicines, you can do with smaller staff in the field and that staff can pay better attention to the specialists. That is how it is more profitable to sell smaller volumes in speciality medicines than in routine sort of products.' This was Dilipbhai's perception and he used this rationale to convince everyone else.

Table 3.1 shows how Sun has improved its ranking in the pharma industry over the years. A break-up of sales by therapy,

TABLE 3.1
Position in the Pharma Industry

Year	Rank	Sun Growth Rate (%)	Industry Growth Rate (%)
1990	70	73	29
1991	57	70	19
1992	48	43	19
1993	44	42	12
1994	34	44	12
1995	30	31	14
1996	28	26	15

Source: Annual Report 1995–96.

regions and main products is given in Table 3.2 and Exhibit 3.1. Selling speciality medicines needs special efforts. You need to know the most pressing but unmet needs of the

TABLE 3.2
Division- and Region-wise Sales

Division	% of Total Sales	Region	% of Total Sales
Aztec Cardiovascular and Diabetic Drug, 145 PSR	29	North	22
Synergy Neuro & Psychiatry Drug	28	South	24
Sun Gastro, Two Major Psychiatry Drugs, Large-volume Drugs	42	East	32
Incare ICU Products, 12 PSR	1	West	22

Source: Annual Report, 1995–96.

EXHIBIT 3.1
Sales of Some Leading Brands of Sun

Rs crore

Sl. No.	Medicine	Sales
1	Monotrate	10
2	Alzolam	6.8
3	Famocid	6.8
4	Angizem	4.1
5	Syndopa	3.8
6	Betatrop	3
7	Carbicef	2.6
8	Lithosun	2.4

Source: ORG Retail Chemist Audit, Dec. 1996.

practitioners. That means you need both the basic familiarity with the discipline as well as thorough familiarity and acceptance among its leading practitioners so as to gauge current needs and problems. You need to look for new molecules that may meet those needs. That requires special expertise, an interfacing skill between the world of practice, the world of pharmacopoeia, the world of research and developments in production technologies, the world of those who manufacture and supply speciality molecules. You have to be able to source these, develop a formulation, test it for normal and accelerated stability, (and/or do the bio-equivalence tests) and obtain clearances from the FDA. This must be done faster than most other potential suppliers, so that you are the first or one of the first few in the market. Sun developed an expertise in this long-drawn process. The company has over a dozen molecules that it was the first to market in the country. It always had a number of practising doctors on its panel as medical advisors. A few doctors have also been employed by Sun. These doctors play several roles. In the first place, they advise Sun about which of the various possible molecules would have the greatest impact on practitioners and hence make sound business sense. Then they help the company in the process of trial, either doing it themselves or liaisoning with hospitals which conduct the trials. They also advise Sun in the selection of research articles and books to be given as gifts. Also, several doctors—experts in their fields—work on the Sunscan service. Let us look at the last two in some detail.

To create and bolster the image of Sun as a company that brings the latest and the best molecule for therapeutic applications, Sun adopted a unique style of promotion. To quote Roy, GM, Synergy, 'The pharma line is used to promotion through professional service representatives (PSRs) who give technical literature, samples and gifts to practitioners. The industry has this practice of sponsoring those doctors to conferences and seminars who use the company's products a lot. The doctors are often too busy to listen to the technical chatter of the PSR and are bored with the humdrum gifts they are given. What would separate us from the others? What could make the doctors welcome our boys? Dilipbhai devised a novel system. He decided to create the image of a company that is far more concerned with the scientific and professional side of the doctor's life than mere business. Right from the beginning, Sun would identify research papers and articles of professional interest to the specialist fraternity, get the reproduction rights and present the copies of the papers to the doctors. This was done time and again. Annual gifts would be current and excellent treatises on a current and topical issue which was gaining a lot of attention of the practitioners and specialists. Our marketing people would give feedback about the issues or themes for the book to be chosen and the panel of doctors would then choose the best among the latest books available. We would get reprint rights of *International Yearbooks*, etc., and give copies to doctors. Again, this was done repeatedly, for years. Any specialist professional's library can be seen to be adorned with books gifted by Sun. Of course, we also had to give the sort of gifts like the competitors 'lest the doctors thought we were miserly.'

'We were the first to start the Continuing Medical Education (CME) programme. What we did was to involve senior and reputed specialists into this along with the local chapter of the Indian Medical Association (or the association of a discipline). The travel and logistics of the senior specialists would be looked after by us. The programme would be conducted under the banner of the Association. We would typically need to hire a hall and arrange for meals and refreshments. We would also put up a stall in a corner with our Company banner. Select general practitioners and younger specialists would be invited as participants to the programme. The specialist would deliver expert talks and then answer questions on some topical medical problems of interest to the invitees. This way we got the goodwill of the Association and its members, of the specialists and the GPs all at one go. And we got it in a very functional and positive manner, which reinforced our reputation of a technically- scientifically-sound company. Later other companies also came forward to sponsor the CMEP. We then moved on to more select talks by specialists for select GPs in smaller halls or banquet rooms of hotels where again our expenditure was low but yielded very high promotional mileage.'

Since about three years, Sun started a service called Sunscan. Any student or researcher in the medical field can write to Sun and request them to send excerpts or abstracts of research papers and documents published in any medical journal anywhere. A team of qualified staff, including some doctors, work on the scan service. When a request is received, the Sunscan team surfs the net and scans the monthly updated CD to identify the right papers, monographs, etc. A bibliography along with the printouts of available abstracts is mailed free of charge to the person making the request. This service is again getting Sun a good deal of favourable attention from the specialist medical community. While many other companies have started this service after Sun, promptitude of response and coverage of the bibliography sent set Sun apart.

Manufacturing and Distribution

Kamlesh Dudhara was the first factory manager of the Vapi unit. His job was to concentrate on manufacturing. The Vapi plant then (as now) had only tablet manufacturing facilities and could not make either capsules, liquids or injectibles. Tablet manufacture is a relatively simple and straightforward process. Preparation of a batch is the first step. This involves the stages of blending, wet granulation, drying, milling and mixing of lubricants. The mixture is then tableted and packed (blister packing, paper strips, opaque or transparent plastic foils, depending upon the medicine's properties—such as sensitivity to light—and the designs chosen by marketing). The quantity of active medicament varies by the formulation. For instance, in Alzolam .25, it is possible to make four tablets a milligram or four thousand tablets in a gram or four million tablets in one kilogram of the active medicament. Such a tablet must be very carefully made, as the medicament is potent. Similar is the case with quite a few psychiatric formulations. This care is largely needed at the stage of mixing the batch. This is always the most critical part of the whole tableting process. While due care is needed for these manufacturing operations, it is not regarded as a very complex process.

The Silvassa plant also concentrates on tablets. The Halol plant of Unimed makes injectibles and capsules. Dudhara, a very talented and accomplished pharmacist, set up the basic processes standards. Manuals and controls in all these plants were set up earlier and have been documented in recent years. He focused on production alone.

What sets apart one company producing high-quality medicines from the rest in the business is the quality-related parameters. These are numerous—reliability of the stated formulation (i.e., does a tablet actually contain the quantity of active medicament it is said to contain), its stability over the claimed shelf-life, the ability to preserve physical and chemical properties in different heat/moisture conditions, etc. These parameters can be tested chemically, spectrographically as well as through chromatography based on the specifications in the pharmacopoeia. Some formulations units try and avoid installation of expensive machines and instruments for these tests. These units perform some simple and inexpensive tests in their premises and get the remaining done outside. Corners are often cut and not every batch is subjected to such tests. This kind of laxity is alleged to be more common in small units which formulate and sell general-purpose OTC medicines (such as anti-pyretics, analgesics, vitamins and antacids).

Partly owing to the nature of its formulations and mainly due to the firm focus on making high-quality medicines, Sun has always been exceptionally meticulous about its manufacturing quality. The Vapi plant still preserves stacks of Quality Control Reports for not only the current batches but also the sold, consumed or expired ones. Sun prides itself on quality. They have installed every kind of expensive equipment and instrument needed to carry out the tests. There are as many as 20 high-precision liquid chromatography (HPLC) machines across different company locations, which can automatically load samples for testing, carry on the tests and print out the results.

Supplies of raw materials, packaging materials, cartons and so on were handled from the Mumbai office earlier by other partners of Sun and now by the team led by Hiren Desai (General Manager) and Harin Mehta (Vice President). Sun has continued for uninterrupted years their business association with the same basic set of suppliers. It has had this system of ensuring suppliers' payments on the contracted due date and delivering the cheque in their office/shop by Sun employees.

One Sun supplier remarked that he has had only one occasion to go to the Sun factory premises for chasing payments and that was in a rare case of incomplete reconciliation of his delivery memos with receipted goods at the stores. Both Hiren Desai and the supplier report that there had never been any underhand deals in Sun. No kickbacks, overinvoicing or things of that kind. Nor was Sun so aggressive as to ban acceptance of normal Diwali gifts by its staff. But the ubiquitous Indian practice of 'cuts' never started here.

Formulations ready for dispatch are stored in a bonded warehouse. Sun maintains a distribution warehouse at Vapi. Dispatch instructions are received through the commercial departments and dispatches carried out from here. The Vapi as well as Silvassa excise matters are looked after together. Sun exports a fair quantity of medicines and the excise duty is refunded on these. It maintains proper documents, hires an excise consultant and does all that is necessary for proper management of dispatch logistics. Sun's approach in this sphere has been quite pragmatic. It has maintained working relationships with staff from Excise, Sales Tax and other such departments.

Sun has appointed C&F agents for distribution. Its commission levels for the distribution chain as well as trade terms follow rather than lead the industry. But payment follow-up is very strict. Habitual late paymasters or those whose instruments are returned are dealt with firmly but politely. The payment position is quite under control, and as can be seen from Exhibits 3.2 and 3.3, the level of trade credits has hovered around two months of sales.

A Place in the Sun

In early 1990, Sun had a major celebration when the company crossed a turnover of Rs 1 crore per month. Today the event appears just one of the milestones, but at that time it was a big hit internally. That was also more or less the time Sun started acting as a company that had come of age. The same year, Sun got converted from a partnership firm called Sun Pharmaceutical Industries to a deemed public limited company called Sun Pharmaceutical Industries Limited. This was done by vesting the property of the partnership firm in the newly registered company by operation of law. This method of conversion avoids costly property transfer stamp duties altogether. Mr Agarwal, General Manager, Legal Department, was of the view that at the time of conversion, the Shanghvi family was better off leaving the firm as a partnership: 'The corporate rate of taxation was 46 per cent and even the highest marginal rate of taxation was smaller than that. And the dividend income for the promoters was certainly going to be taxed again, so from a taxation point of view, conversion was not a very profitable idea.'

The reason they the family went in for the conversion was Dilipbhai's perception, shared by several of his executives, that Sun was going to be a large corporate giant and could not be expected to be managed in the culture of a partnership firm. Things had to become professionalised, systematic, independent of the promoters. There was a lot of internal discussion on this issue. The other persons who had worked

EXHIBIT 3.2
Condensed Profit & Loss Statements for Year Ended 31 March

Rs lakh

	1990	1991	1992	1993	1994	1995	1996
Sales	972	1,457	2,459	3,138	5,131	9,211	13,017
Other Income	2	9	54	87	115	174	89
Materials	423	619	1,202	1,625	2,649	4,259	5,120
Excise	127	169	210	257	282	915	1,349
Personnel	66	93	151	238	328	557	788
Op. Cost	243	396	534	662	1,004	1,355	1,870
Interest	11	17	60	111	128	0	0
Depreciation	13	37	13	19	35	117	279
PBT	91	135	343	313	820	2,179	3,697
Tax	0	0	35	61	82	35	0
Adjustments	0	0	31	1	6	0	0
PAT	91	135	339	253	744	2,144	2,179

Source: Prospectus issued in 1994 and Annual Reports thereafter.

EXHIBIT 3.3
Condensed Balance Sheet as on 31 March

Rs lakh

	1993	1994	1995	1996
Share Capital (Incl. of Bal. in Shareholders A/c)	641	719	1,476	1,480
Reserves	28	956	7,902	11,284
Secured Loans	641	1,478	1,476	1,761
Unsecured Loans	211	223	53	48
Current Liabilities & Provisions	394	1,001	1,669	2,354
	1,915	4,377	12,576	16,927
Gross Block	676	1,861	3,692	5,856
Depreciation	53	888	205	483
Net Block	623	1,773	3,486	5,260
CWIP	11	220	29	15
Investments	2	2	3	7
Inventories	524	1,057	1,333	3,030
Debtors	560	742	1,541	2,036
Cash & Bank	24	127	527	263
Deferred Expenses			87	59
Loans & Advances	171	456	5,254	5,549

Source: Prospectus issued in 1994 and Annual Reports thereafter.

with Dilipbhai to make the partnership firm a huge success decided to move out. This separation occurred between 1993 and 1995. 'There was no bitterness or rancour. I can introduce you to them and set up meetings with my ex-partners. Even when we joined hands in the early 1980s, we had agreed that we must work together only till such time as we feel that we are meeting our shared objectives. I am not working in Sun merely to earn more money. By God's grace, I have made a bit. I have a dream about this company. My partners had different personal objectives, different ways of relaxing, of enjoying the fruit of their hard work, different work style and different perception of what this company meant to their personal lives. We are still very good friends. Naturally our intensity of interaction has decreased as we have taken different paths, but we remain family friends, visiting each other and sharing with each other our moments of happiness.' This is how Dilipbhai recounts the separation of his partners from Sun.

The 'copy and sell till someone copies you' manner of the growth of the Indian pharmaceutical industry was very common in the 1980s. Even the most established names had but perfunctory research facilities. Given the size of the company, it was thus quite an unusual decision when Sun built its R&D centre called Sparc at Vadodara, inaugurated by the Vice-President of India in 1993. Sparc now works for developing and testing formulations, for therapeutic applications and for developing processes for manufacturing active medicaments/drugs. It may be noted that the research facilities of many other companies came up after Sun's.

The public issue of the company was a celebration in itself. The company made the public issue more, it would appear retrospectively, to claim its arrival as a full-fledged pharma marketing company in the Indian market. It was more a declaration of adulthood than an effort to garner public money through crafty campaigning as the Indian commercial world is wont to do. The company issued 3.7 million shares of Rs 10 each at a premium of Rs 150 per share. The issue was oversubscribed and the company generated Rs 592 million from the issue. The money itself was not so important as the recognition of its inner strength by a market that had been cheated time and again by opportunistic promoters since 1991–92. The company gave loans to its own employees to help them buy shares in the company. Practically ever since its public issue, Sun has had a surplus cash position and its net interest costs are negative, according to Mr Baheti, Vice President (Finance). Sun has an asset base of Rs 1,457 million (cost/book) of which the debt component is under Rs 176 million. When asked why they are so conservative in financing, one was told that this was not being conservative but being focused. They had no need for money at the moment as they did not have projects of the type they wished to invest in. 'Why should we take more loans? I know we can get as much funds from the market as the next company, but what do we do with them? We do not want to invest in lines other than our own and we are not in the banking business either!' was how Baheti put it. In fact when Sun bought a stake in M.J. Pharma or in Gujarat Lyka, they did so by paying out solid cash, not by swapping shares of the two companies. As Baheti told us, 'The Sun equity is very precious and its value is rising by the minute. We are not going to dilute it like that. In fact the only time we thought we allowed someone to get our equity cheap was when TDICI got a block for financing our projects at Panoli and Silvassa as well as Sparc.'

From about 1995–96, Sun has gone on an acquisition spree. It first acquired the Boots plant at Nagar and started manufacturing 5 ASA, Tramadol and other medicines in that plant. Then it took a stake in M.J. Pharma. Then came a stake in Gujarat Lyka Organics. A stake was also acquired in a US company called Caraco for expanding Sun's presence in the US generic medicine business, a component which is expected to become increasingly important in its future growth. Finally in 1997 came the merger with Tamilnadu Dadha. Sun clearly wishes to emerge as one of the largest (if not the largest) pharmaceutical marketing companies in the country. There is a serious plan to float a petrochemical company a couple of years down the line, to make the basic raw materials for some of the bulk drugs made by Sun. To quote Dilipbhai, 'Our petrochemical venture should not be thought as being the same type as Reliance or MRPL. We are joining hands with IPCL for making some chemicals by hydrocarbon route. These chemicals will be used for making bulk drugs which we can either sell or use for formulations. It is not a wholly unrelated diversification, but a further backward integration of sorts.' The new company would be set up by Dilip Shanghvi in his personal capacity, not through Sun.

Sustaining the Growth

A common refrain heard from many senior officers in Sun was that they have been growing very fast and that the pace of growth has put tremendous pressures on the systems. They need to consolidate, not so much in financial terms but organisationally. Absence of this has led to glitches and waste in the past. A young executive told me how once there was this 'Project C-form' under which a team of three–four executives spent months trying to collect, put together and reconcile all the C-forms required for all the intra-state sales transaction for a few years. The amount involved was a few crore.

Dilipbhai realised by about the early 1990s that Sun could no longer continue to make moves only on the basis of one person's views. A greater degree of systematic teamwork was necessary. He candidly admits making several mistakes due to this somewhat unsystematic and high-pressure work culture prevailing then. 'We should have introduced several medicines about which we got indications from the market or our people, and which would have made our company much larger than what it is today. We missed these. And then we introduced products which did not do well and took away our efforts. Why, once I even made bulk drugs in a formulations unit, something one cannot do well and should never have happened if I had our current method of working.'

The formalisation of the organisation began some time in 1992. Till then, Dilipbhai was accessible to a large number of officers for guidance and decision making. He is still available but matters have increasingly been delegated to different officers as hierarchies have become stable and reporting lines drawn up. New people have been joining. The consolidation efforts have been underway since 1994.

In 1994, Sun created four marketing divisions for handling the now numerous products. Synergy division focuses on neuropsychiatry therapies. Sun focuses on gastro-intestinal medicines. Aztec concentrates on cardiovascular drugs.

Finally, INCA focuses on speciality medicines needed in intensive care and in surgical applications. The logic of divisionalisation was to facilitate a degree of specialisation among the salesforce, speciality-oriented customer focus and better market planning at management levels. 'Now in the same city we have several PSRs. It is quite possible that more than one PSR may visit the same doctor. This creates no confusion as the two will be talking about different drugs altogether. Now every salesperson can focus only on a select group of practitioners and a related group of medicines. Training becomes simpler. The promotional message is more focused. Better attention can now be given to practitioners. That is why divisionalisation has been done.'

The company started moving slowly towards formal budgetary controls in 1995. Baheti as Vice President, Finance, is responsible for institutionalising a complete management control system. He stated that they wished to finally implement a full-fledged profit-centre type of control system: 'We had quite an informal system of decision making. Though we had a transparent and proper system of accounts, people did not have budgets to worry about. We had to first start identifying the various elements of expenses being incurred at the department level. While we keep centralised accounts, we started informing departmental heads of the monthly expenditure on each of the important head. Then we started moving towards getting budgets prepared. I still do not see this as a very rigid budgetary control system, departments can still seek and get substantial mid-period changes. But we are moving. Eventually we will have a responsibility-centre system where a manager will be responsible either for a profit centre or a cost centre and become accountable for performance vis à vis budget. We are doing our own system development, training people, counselling them, negotiating on procedural matters, etc., so that our managers do not feel threatened. We could have hired a consultant for this job but we believe that an externally devised system will be thought of as an imposition. Our officers now feel that what we will have is their own system.'

Yagnik, Vice President, HRD, described how the consolidation process is taking shape. He himself joined in 1989 when the company was very small. Slowly, he started formalising the HRD matters. Today his biggest task is in managing the human relations in this rapidly growing organisation. So far, Sun has had very smooth industrial relations. There was only one industrial dispute in the Vapi plant. 'We could sort out the matters through talking across the table. They really did not have any genuine grievances, wages were better than most of the units around us then and our approach had always been friendly. The matter was sorted out. Thereafter we never had any industrial dispute,' says Yagnik. 'Previously people could approach Dilipbhai or Nitinbhai directly and have their problems addressed. These could be work-related or otherwise. Now we have to report to our boss, who in turn reports to his boss, who in turn may report to a VP who in turn... etc. We feel as if our importance has decreased here. We understand that as Sun becomes larger, this is bound to happen, but we feel that the old touch is drying up' is how one employee expressed himself. Yagnik is aware of this: 'We have chosen a deliberate path of ensuring closer and smoother interaction between executives at various levels and the staff members. This is done in a very functional way, in seminars in which employees share the good things they have done with each other, through training programmes, through *Sunmilan* and other ways.'

Yagnik said that the company believes in allowing its people to reach their full potential. It focuses on functional training. The training programmes are mostly handled internally. That way the trainer and the trainee, both employees of the company, come closer and the trainer gets an opportunity to share his learning with others. Some training programmes are also handled by external consultants. Regular seminars are also organised on new ideas and work done by people.

Virtually anyone can speak at this forum and all are welcome to attend. This event has gained popularity and people feel good talking about what they did. There is the feeling of being recognised by peers and the company.

Sun arranges annual/biannual conferences of management personnel on specific management themes. For cultivating the feeling of belonging to a family, *Sunmilan*, a social get-together of all the employees and their families is organised once a year. Cultural events, picnics and games mark the event, fully paid for by the company. The company also publishes an in-house journal called *Sunvaad* which is instrumental in sharing the achievements and views across the staff.

Interpretation of Actions at Sun and the Inferences Drawn

Marketing

From the very beginning, Sun marketed speciality medicines. It chose psychotropic drugs to start with in Bengal. Initially, Shanghvi used his social network in the pharma trade extensively. Simultaneously, he also developed some useful but unobtrusive social contacts with leading medical practitioners in the field. He was inquisitive and curious from his college days and after entering business, he seems to have made his curiosity purposive—about how do which doctors prescribe medicines to whom. Psychotropic drugs have two advantages for the marketer: they offer perhaps the highest margins to the seller and second, they are needed in long-run therapy. 'It is not like ampicillin, where there are hundreds of brands available and a particular patient's requirement is over in a week,' said an insider of the trade.

Shanghvi's happy experience with speciality medicines (psychotropic drugs) required in long-term therapy possibly induced him to generalise on that as his basic approach for picking up products. General-purpose medicines (such as antibiotics, antipyretics, analgesics, antacids, tonics and vitamins) are recommended by a large number of general practitioners to an even larger number of patients. Their demand might vary seasonally (e.g., the medicines for curing upper respiratory tract ailments are more in demand during the monsoon when the whole world sneezes). Speciality medicines are recommended by a smaller set of specialists. They more or less conclusively influence the actual buyer behaviour of the patients. Seldom does one think of questioning a specialist's judgement. Once a patient starts on one medicine, he seldom changes it till the nature of his malady changes. (For example, my doctor recommended a certain preparation for my hypertension six years ago. I continue taking the same drug even now. And there are millions who behave exactly like this.) Sun's marketing strategy revolved around this realisation and hence on making *first the company and then the product wanted* by the specialists. Its products were of very high quality, reliable and consistent. Packaging was nothing special. No one in Sun talked about their medicines being affordably priced. Other pharma companies make a lot of fuss about the 'reasonable price' of their drugs. This is not to say that Sun's products were exorbitantly priced, but that price was not used as a strategy to win marketshare. Sun's distribution system initially relied on Shanghavi's social network and later followed rather than led the industry practice. The unique style of promotion through Continuing Medical Education (CME) programmes first adopted by Sun was very effective. The strategy of repeatedly giving thoughtfully designed gifts in the form of copies of current editions of journals/books or monograms on highly complex and professionally exciting topics was a masterstroke. Developing an image of scientifically oriented company thus became a core concept in its marketing strategy. The Sun-scan service to medical researchers distinguished it from other companies and reinforced this message. These efforts of promotion were crucial to the company success. They gave Sun a unique image in the minds of the doctors. Doctors started 'looking forward to the visit of our salesmen to see what new information or paper he would bring rather that our salesmen having to wait for the doctors to give them time'. The salesmen were heard, the company remembered and well thought of. This was then the answer to their search for competitive edge. I thus credit this strategy of special and innovative promotion, subtle and generalised to the level of the company (rather than blunt and product-specific) as being responsible for Sun's initial success.

By establishing close links with the relevant medical practitioners, Sun was able to be ahead of the market. It could anticipate the problems faced by the specialists and identify the specific unmet needs of a therapy. Through its panel of medical advisers, the company proactively searched for molecules that offered the solutions to these felt needs of practitioners. Even as a small company, it developed, tested and introduced the concerned formulation. And this it did time and again. It has brought out a steady stream of drugs sold for the first time in India by any one. Almost each time it grew in sales and profits. And yet Shanghvi admitted to having made many mistakes: of not choosing certain new products as well as of having chosen some in the hope that they would grow.

Sun's promotion activity deserves emphasis and repetition. It is unique. Though followed by many others now, it was then innovative. The promotion tack is given in detail in the case above. Sun sold itself as a company having high concern for professional excellence, as wishing to bring in the latest and the best in the therapy to the practice. It caught the prospective specialists young. This it did through Sunscan and also by donating expensive books to libraries of medical colleges. As one executive claimed, the young aspirant specialist found that several times the examination questions would be based on materials discussed in 'Sun's' books (that is, books donated by Sun). It was perhaps the first to start the CME programmes on private initiative. And to cap it all, it started the Sunscan service for helping researchers and students to access current literature. This is truly a unique form of promotion in pharma marketing where expensive gifts, sponsorships of trips abroad and liquor-and-dinner style of promotion dominates.

Finance

Capital Structure

Sun started with a small capital base of about Rs one lakh and formal loans from banks etc., of about Rs 10 lakh, including personal loans of about Rs six lakh taken by Shanghvi. The company systematically reinvested operational surpluses, so that by the time it became a public limited company (some 10 years down the line), its equity base became about Rs six crore. Personal loans were taken well up to the mid 1980s for meeting working capital needs, for their flexibility and ease of access. The increase in equity through retained earnings was thus Rs 590 lakh out of 600! By then, it had taken formal institutional finance twice: Rs 60 lakh in 1988 and Rs 300 lakh in 1990. The debt–equity ratio has been conservative, 1.3 debt for 1 equity in 1994 (industry average at 2.5). By this time, personal loans were no longer needed for the management of the company. Since 1994, due to its IPO at a very high premium, the company is cash surplus and there was some talk of negative interest cost.

Some calculations show the leverage figures as below:

	1990	1991	1992	1993	1994	1995	1996
Operating Leverage	1.13	1.24	1.03	1.04	1.04	1.05	1.00
Financial Leverage	1.12	1.13	1.17	1.35	1.16	1.00	1.00
Total Leverage	1.26	1.40	1.21	1.42	1.20	1.05	1.00

This is a remarkably conservative financing of a business. One can understand it post-IPO considering it had obtained the funds at a large premium, and its effect does show on reduced leverage post-1994. But even before that, the company finances were managed very conservatively. Thus to add to Dilip Shanghvi's stated desire to limit the risk on either the technology or the market side, there has been this consistent desire to avoid financial risks.

EXHIBIT 3.4
Sourcing and Use of Funds

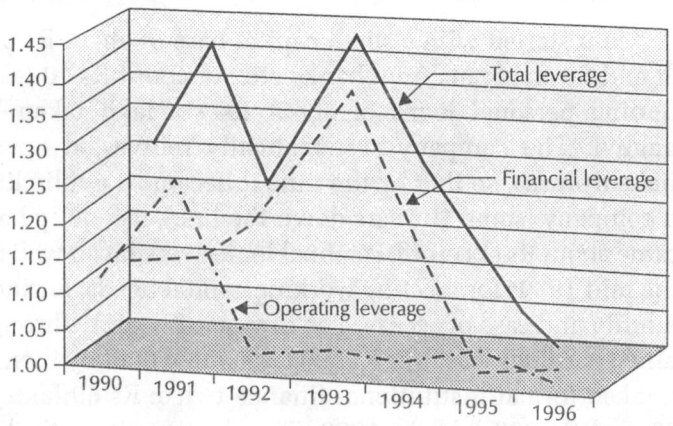

Till 1994, the funds used were either internal accruals or personal as well as formal institutional loans. The first and only IPO happened in 1994. Funds were deployed till 1990 almost evenly between fixed and current assets. By 1993, fixed assets soaked up Rs 639 lakh as compared to working capital of Rs 882 lakh. As of the last reported figures, the capital funds of Rs 1,840 million (150 million equity, 1,276 million retained surpluses and 180 million in loans in addition to some 240 million in current liabilities) were applied thus: 530 million in fixed assets and balance in current assets. Thus the company has consistently ensured that its working capital needs do not suffer for want of funds.

Managing Working Capital

Between 1993 and 1996, years for which data is available, the inventories varied between 1.7 to 2 months sales, rising in the last year. The pharma industry average has been between 61 and 72 days as per CMIE (*India's Corporate Sector*, April 1998, p. 220) The debtors remained consistently around two months of sales, reducing marginally towards the 1996 (industry average 43–56 days during these years). The company apparently used moderate inventories and longer credit periods as a way of securing higher sales. This was facilitated by relatively high margins on products (consistently over 100 per cent on materials consumed—the industry average of raw material cost as proportion of sales has been between 58 and 60 per cent) and a prudently designed capital structure. Thus despite high levels of working capital, interest costs were simply not a worry, nor was liquidity in question.

Pace of Expansion

When Sun started operations from Gujarat, the company already had an established market for its products in the East. It had established this by getting their products manufactured in third-party premises. It thus started in Gujarat by creating a factory to meet own needs. The first factory was in a tiny *gala* in GIDC, Vapi. It was an unassuming little factory. Today it appears cramped. Sun's original unit in Vapi, built in 1982, had to be expanded almost immediately to house the quality control department. Sun expanded the facilities twice before 1985, as sales grew quickly. This expansion was done in an incremental manner: adding a blender here, a grinder there and a packaging line somewhere in between. Then came a sister company—Unimed—managed by Sun. This was a full-blown factory at Halol. Sun's own expansions seem to have followed sales growth and not lead it. Till well into the 1990s, Sun relied on several third-party manufacturing contracts to augment its own production facilities for meeting the sales targets. This picture continues throughout. In its later life, Sun set up one bulk drug unit at Panoli and a formulations unit at Silvassa. It acquired facilities of the companies in which it took a controlling interest and also bought one plant of an MNC. Sun does not give the image of a manufacturing-dominated organisation wherein marketing has to function overtime to ensure capacity utilisation. It is the other way round. The approach of Sun in choosing a mode is pragmatic (making the best use of available resources) rather than absolute (pitting for the technologically most sophisticated option).

Efforts to Reduce Costs/Improve Efficiency

Sun has never been a production-dominated company. Its strength lay in its market position and not in its production costs. Sun competed well not on account of low cost positions but superb market creation and nurturing efforts. Executives I spoke to never particularly stressed on efforts at painstaking process improvements for better material recovery or lower utilities consumption. Relatively speaking, these efforts were more pronounced in case of the logistics of purchase of materials (including active medicaments for the psychotropic drugs). Bootstrapping was attempted in distribution logistics as well. A senior manager in Sun said that identifying the best sources of active medicament was clearly a competitive strength of Sun. The importance of distribution logistics became more pronounced as the distribution activity had to cope with several sources of medicines in the Sun fold, including third-party factories, and hundreds of 'sinks' or destinations (C&F depots, etc.). This happened particularly after a trauma connected with some sales tax documentation due to a system that had started cracking up under extra load.

What Did I Find Special About Management Processes in Sun?

- Even as a very small formulation unit, Sun not only undertook simpler tests in its QC laboratory, but also acquired expensive machines such as the HPLC. One seldom sees such equipment with SSI formulators. And this in Vapi's ethos, a town thickly populated with SSI formulators. Cut-throat competition among formulators is and has been the order of the day here. As one Sun officer put it, the single most important factor contributing to Sun's growth was its unwavering commitment to high quality.
- While Sun also did follow the usual promotion practices of offering useful gifts and services to medical practitioners, it created an image for itself as a company deeply interested in its therapy in scientific terms.
- It contributed a great deal towards upgrading the knowledge of the profession through its Continuing Education Programme.
- It helped many to stay current with the recent advances in their field by way of monographs, books and journals.
- It also contributed such literature to libraries of colleges so that it was in a position to create a favourable image among the new entrants to the profession.
- By constant monitoring of the developments in the therapy, Sun developed a system of identifying the felt needs of the medical professionals and searching for molecules that met that need. This way, it kept a flow of amazingly regular new product introductions.
- To top it all, it was a remarkably bold decision for a company its size to take up serious process and product development.

Sun started as a single-therapy formulation company, added two other therapies almost after a decade, added a surprisingly (surprising for a company of that size in 1992) expensive R&D and then went on a buying spree acquiring companies after a major success in its IPO. It has a formidable position to day due to its innovative product choice and marketing practices.

The company took these innovative steps in its search for cost-effective ways of marketing its products. The basic question was how could a small company, not possessing the same reputation for technical expertise or marketing strengths as a large multinational company with which it must compete, do so. Why would its products be prescribed by leading professionals of medical specialities? Why would the specialists take the salesmen seriously? How could the company create a special position for itself? Dilip Shanghvi grappled with these questions along with his marketing team. Initially, he had a lot of time which he used to learn about the therapies, know the doctors, discuss with his friends in the medical profession about how to do these things and discover issues and problems. The strategy of focusing on a single therapy for compact and efficient operations maintaining better contacts with practitioners thus emerged. As did the strategy of keeping therapy-wise marketing divisions so as to continue to enjoy the same advantages even after the company had become multi-therapy medicine marketer.

Did Sun Commit any Blunders?

To start with, Sun was dependent on only the East Indian market for psychotropic drugs, which is how the company began. It shifted to Vapi because the management thought that this established pharma belt was a better place for a pharma company. It systematically reduced its dependence on the East Indian market and then on one therapy. Thus over time, it achieved a degree of product and market diversification. No blunder here.

The company had been adding fixed assets quickly but incrementally and never so dramatically as to cause a liquidity crunch. No blunder here again. It certainly did not speculate on raw material prices and the like. There is no evidence of Sun doing informal, cash business. So no blunders here either.

Yes, they floated more than one firm. The Halol company (Unimed) was set up as a separate firm, there is a distribution company and an export company. The logic was that the Halol firm, owned by relatives and friends in which Shanghvi himself has little stake, is used as a production base and the dealings are on the same terms as with other third-party suppliers. There was a possibility of them joining him in making Sun bigger, but then there was the potential loss of Sun's SSI status and in 1985 it was a consideration. But brands, market strength and corporate image were built and no effort was squandered. And everything was managed in an above-board manner. Sun did not commit any of the other blunders either.

Analysis of the Strategy Followed by Sun

Product Market Posture

Sun began by offering drugs in psychotherapy. For several years it restricted itself to that. Then it added drugs to be used in cardiovascular therapy and in treating intestinal maladies. More recently, it offered life-saving products required in critical care. All Sun products are thus ethical drugs prescribed by specialists and, in most cases, needed by patients on a regular, long-term basis. This set of products was chosen based on the earlier positive experience with this strategy.

Growth Vector

Sun introduced more and more drugs in the same therapy when it was restricting its scope to psychotropic drugs. Later the company moved from 'therapy to therapy', that is, it retained the same basic option of speciality medicines but for reasons of growth, chose a different speciality.

Once chosen, the number of drugs in the same therapy was multiplied for a fuller range. This was a form of widening the product line in the broad ethical drug field. With the establishment of its R&D laboratory, the company also introduced new, 'first-time-in-India' products in each speciality. This further strengthened its presence in each therapy. Finally, it started marketing bulk drugs as well. This was at times an unrelated diversification. (It is not clear whether the company marketed the bulk drugs used in its own formulations, i.e., whether the marketing was merely a way of utilising the bulk-drug units to their full capacity. There was also the business of exports. Thus the growth vector was a combination of product line widening, vertical integration and geographical expansion.

Competitive Edge Developed

The company developed a competitive edge by two distinct means. One was creating a corporate image in the minds of prescribing doctors through a series of steps. The second was developed by continuous efforts at new-products introduction, for which the company kept a panel of doctors who recommended a new drug, assisted in its testing and release, etc.

After its IPO, Sun also used its surplus liquidity as a competitive edge in buying up or acquiring controlling interests in pharma companies, giving it the advantage of low-cost and speedy-expansion manufacturing base.

Synergy Deployed

Sun's ability to develop a rapport with leading specialists of a particular therapy to create and develop its technical sales and promotion competence for catering to them was its chief synergy. Its corporate image in the medical fraternity, the expertise in identifying opportunities for new product introductions and the ability to complete all the testing- and release-related formalities before competitors were other elements of synergies across products.

Perception of Core Competence

Sun appears to perceive its core competence in marketing of high-quality drugs needed in long-term treatment of select diseases. It also uses its competence in new-product introduction.

Logic and Duration of Flirtation with New Activities

Sun has virtually never strayed from areas of its core competence. Only recently has it entered drugs that are needed for immediate rather than long-term treatment, but this is a minor digression—if one were to consider it as such—from its consistent stand. The marketing of bulk drugs undertaken by it is possibly to use up the slack in production facilities.

Sun's strategy has thus revolved around:

- establishing a strong image in the specialist medical fraternity
- identifying new products that would meet the felt need of such specialist medical community, these drugs usually being needed for long-term treatment
- integrating vertically in certain medicines
- using inexpensively obtained money to build manufacturing capacity through acquisitions, indicating a strong focus on core competence

Organisational Issues

Changes in the Organisation Structure

Sun underwent reorganisation in its marketing set-up when it became a multi-therapy company. Marketing is now organised into four divisions, each handling a certain specified product group. This was done to achieve focus. Overall, the organisation seems to be in a state of flux and the structural response to the series of acquisitions is anything but complete.

Sun's personnel policy has stressed careful selection of employees to ensure that they would fit in the 'Sun way of doing things.' This involves the ability to work hard, under pressure and in teams; it demands trust, collaborative behaviour and openness. Sun has not gone out of its way to hire 'live wire, aggressive go-getters'. Its recruitment ads have for several years carried the line 'Join the winning team', emphasising 'team' as much as 'winning'. That a large majority of Sun staff are from Gujarat does not indicate a regional preference, but a natural pattern, the Executive Assistant to Shanghvi being from Orissa. Several key executives are non-Gujarati. Compensation at Sun is superior to the prevailing market rates in Vadodara.

The management process seems to be in a state of flux, caused by three factors. The first was the reorganisation in divisions, the second that an increased degree of formalisation was now demanded. The third was the fact that new companies/facilities were being added very rapidly. As a result, there was the inevitable degree of sullenness in older employees who felt the distance between them and their immediate bosses. Sun has been internally developing formal control procedures and adopting the modern concepts of profit centres in its control systems. This again emphasises the desire for team effort, for transparency and trust between people while at the same time moving towards formalisation.

4

Marketing in the Successful Companies

Possibly due to the proliferation of business writing about new products and advertisements, the word 'marketing' brings to mind fast-moving consumer goods (FMCG). It is as if FMCG marketing is the only marketing activity worth talking about. Since virtually none of the companies I studied are in the FMCG line (Does that tell us something about the chances of new entrepreneurs growing big on the strength of an FMCG?), what I write about marketing may not be exactly in tune with what one reads in the *Brand Equity* supplement of *The Economic Times*. After all, marketing activity begins with the very choice of what one makes, goes on to define the four *P*s and then gets enmeshed in the morass of salesforce and distribution channel management. The last bit is usually considered too dusty and prosaic to be talked about in marketing discussions, though it forms the backbone of the function. So I will talk about these three facets as well and then, above all, the lessons one learns about how to compete in the market.

Choice of Products

Many readers are likely to argue that the marketing function begins well after one has decided what products to sell. By itself, it does not determine the products. This is undoubtedly so for an established enterprise. But if one were to start a new enterprise or, having started, were to start afresh, the following discussion would be of help.

In my discussions with small-industry owners, I have often heard that they chose a particular 'line' because it was that of a 'running item' (in Hindi, a *chalnewala* item). By this they mean that the need for the product is widely felt, that hence they do not need to create an awareness about it, that there possibly are numerous sellers of similar products and that the demand for the product is large and, like for diamonds, forever. This then is the classic case of an entrepreneur introducing a 'me too' product, trying to get a small piece of an established market. And depending upon how central is the question of quality in buyer behaviour, what the advantages are of being a local rather than a national player, what the proportion of transportation cost is in the total cost, etc., one might succeed. That too, often on grounds of price and trade discount rather than on quality, superior features or things like that. Such a choice of the product happens to be that of a typical mercantile capitalist who has strayed into industry from trade. In my observation this he does in the lizard style (See 'A matter of style' in *How Not to Ruin Your Small Industry*.) While this is the choice of those who survive, it is unlikely to lead to spectacular or even reasonably quick growth.

And one can see why. The enterprise starts by catering to an existing demand created by someone else. Therefore, the product is at best 'just as good' as the 'original', only locally made and possibly a bit cheaper. And there are many other lizards also making and selling similar products. The demand for such an established product is usually not growing any faster than at demographic rates, certainly not at dramatic rates (there could be some exceptions such as software education, which has become a *chalnewala* item and is still growing rapidly). The entrepreneur must therefore engage in a 'market share' game, possibly using physical proximity, credit periods, trade discounts and price as tools. The volume of business in these lines has a tendency to be controlled by the amount of working capital one has. Since that is expensive, the total volume one can handle is limited. Fast growth is unlikely, but the business can be stable. A person who wishes to be his or her own boss may choose a running item; an entrepreneur who wishes to grow big may not be making a brilliant decision by doing the same.

It should not surprise you therefore that virtually every company studied had started with a product/service which was either new or was in the growth phase of its product life cycle. (It is believed in marketing metaphysics that every—or almost every—product has a life cycle. When it is introduced for the first time in any market, buyers need to be made aware of it. Only the adventurous types—the innovators—who wish to be associated with new and fancy things choose to buy it. Once a certain track record is established, the next-rung people, those who are alert and aware but also prudent, take to it. This class, called the early adopters, is larger than the innovators' class and hence the demand for the product rises. Then the ordinary folk take to it after having seen and heard about many people, including possibly their role models and social superiors, using it. This class is even larger and is called the late adopters. When the product reaches this class, its demand starts tapering off. Now only the laggards remain—either the poor country cousins who are reached well after the more accessible city elites have been served, or the people who buy a Rubik's cube for their children when all their cousins have broken theirs!—Incidentally, in India, for several products, the class of rural and country cousins is still very large and that is the famous promise of rural marketing. Finally some substitute product appears on the scene and the focal product becomes outdated or unacceptable. This total span from the introduction to the eventual demise is called the product life cycle—PLC.)

To be specific:

Sumangal innovated and introduced *Kalnirnaya*, the first almanac-cum-calendar in the Maharashtra market. (It appears that a somewhat similar product made by Bangalore Press was in vogue in Karnataka for a long time prior to *Kalnirnaya*. But in Maharashtra, it was certainly a new product.) Later, *Kaldarshak, Tithitoran* and a whole lot of other me-too products came in. Sumangal started selling these calendars at a time when every house used to get free calendars from the grocer, clothier or insurance agent. The product concept itself was new and Sumangal's creative product design and marketing strategy created a new market. *Kalnirnaya* came out at the very start of the PLC of this new product category.

DRL time and again introduced bulk drugs that were relatively new in Indian markets. These drugs were, prior to being produced in India, imported at high prices due to the tariffs. Once DRL introduced these at lower prices, many more formulations based on these appeared and the total demand for the drug grew rapidly. This they did for Metronidazole in 1973, Sulphametaxazole in 1978, Methyldopa in 1984 and Quinolones in 1988. Each product was chosen when it was either new or at an early growth stage in its PLC. DRL moved out of each one of these—and picked up another new one—when the domestic competition among the bulk drugs makers for the product increased.

Praj started by introducing the continuous-type fermentation process equipment for molasses-based distilleries attached to sugar mills. Till they came in a big way, most of the distilleries were using batch-type technologies. Soon, those who set up new distilleries (and in a spirited country, there are quite a few) began to prefer the continuous-type process and thus the product's growth phase began. Praj chose a product at its growth phase.

When Mastek started its software developing business in India, the whole field of software applications in the business world was budding in India. Mastek was among the early ones who prospered with the growth of the software applications industry. It was also the first to capitalise on the proliferation of desktop PCs by introducing among the first 'canned' packages in the country, namely FINAC and STRAC. Again, when the RDBMS thing had yet to take root in the country, Mastek came in quickly with their Ingress-based solutions and captured a big slice of the domestic institutional market. That service is now towards the phase-out part of its PLC.

Biocon started with isinglass, an established and old product. But the company would never have been talked about had it not come up with the enzymes for which it is known. The enzyme, meant for textiles (stonewashing of jeans), came at its growth phase, piggyriding as it were on the growth of the denim industry. As was the case with many other products too.

V-Guard caught the fluctuating mood of the state power supply and piggyrode on the growth of consumer durables such as refrigerators and televisions. The product, voltage stabilisers, was certainly at its growth phase in the late 1970s. That was well before products with built-in voltage stabilising components came in the market. And among the regrets which the company has is having missed the growth phase of constant voltage transformers for computers!

Sun proactively searched for molecules whose therapeutic powers seemed to offer solutions to the felt needs of practitioners, and developed and introduced the concerned formulation time and again. The company is known for the steady stream of 'first time in India' drugs, growing each time in sales and profits.

Though not a new class of drugs (in fact over 20 years old), cephalosporins had a large potential in the world market and hence were still in the growth phase when Orchid started making them. Not just far but actually remote from their phase-out stage as at least half of those who cough away in this country will vouch!

And so it goes for almost every company. In summary, the companies in our study, chosen for their relatively rapid growth and transition out of small industry status, seem to have done one remarkable thing in common: *they picked up products that were at the growth phase of their respective PLC.*

It is not difficult to see why this should facilitate growth. If the product is at its growth phase, then the market itself is rising. And in such a growing market, an early entrant has a bright chance of picking up a good market share at a comfortable margin. The characteristics of the market can be studied and the possibility of specialising in one segment where the unit would have near monopoly realised. Since all the players are trying to get their share of a growing cake, they are not so interested in a business where they see an expert player, but in segments where they can have free passage. Thus the dangers of a price war are not significant. The buyers too are possibly not excessively preoccupied with price since there still possibly is an element of novelty and the comparison is with an option that is now considered somewhat anachronistic. To illustrate, when new, people were willing to pay a much higher price for inkjet printers since the comparison was with the conventional dot matrix printers and the quality advantage of shifting to inkjet was distinctly visible. These advantages sort of evaporate once a lot of me-too lizards identify the product as a *chalnewala* item and start crowding the market.

What is important is to identify products that are in the growth phase of their respective PLC and also within the competence of the firm seeking to make them. The products do not have to be new or innovative, though by definition innovative products will be at the growth phase of their PLC. But for innovative products, there is much too high a risk and the element of chance can be overbearing. In our sample, the only truly 'innovative' product was *Kalnirnaya*. (While the continuous fermentation technology as well as the use of Dual Route developed by Praj were innovations too, they are the same as the use of cellulose in stonewashing of jeans developed by Biocon, FINAC of Mastek and other first-in-India products/processes.) Other companies did not introduce wholly new products, but introduced products whose market was growing. That is possibly easier. Entrepreneurs are not and should not exclusively be inventors!

The question then is how does one identify which products are at the growth phase of their PLC. This question is not easy to answer. One needs to understand the market and the industry thoroughly, and to obtain a realistic projection about the likely trends in terms of technology development as well as consumer preferences in the industry. This would be based on what the user industry (in case of an industrial intermediate product) feels about its future requirement, what the industry trends elsewhere suggest, what one may judge about the consumer behaviour in this country, etc. Serious judgement would be involved. Should you not spend time and money thinking about and analysing these things before making a project proposal rather than rushing around with one for persuading unfortunate bankers to part with their resources? It seems this is what successful companies and their promoters do. Shanghvi was explicit about it when he said, 'I had much time and little money, hence I had to use my time well.' Choudhary of Praj went through an elaborate search and product identification procedure to identify his particular line. Mastek rejected management consulting—though it was meant in their initial name—as well as some other lines. Others took up more than one line and then focused on the one that was in the growth phase of its PLC. But the question about how to identify products in the growth phase of their PLC still remains only partially answered. I have indicated elements to that answer and they all point to the fact that this aspect needs a lot of effort—much more than buying a ready-to-submit project report!

The decision to choose a product in the growth phase of its PLC is obviously risky. When I was a student, we were told that only one in 52 new products succeeds. The number '52' often made me feel that whosoever made this statement regarded the choice of products like finding the trump ace in a pack of cards. Perhaps this proportion has gone up even further. Allegorically one is right though stochastically one may be optimistic! The risks are about being before one's right time, about having to go through an elaborate consumer education period, about having overestimated the market, about even encountering hitherto unexplored legal issues, etc. Any of these risks could entail failure. It is not as if these successful companies invariably picked up only winners. For example, Dr Reddy's also started making cephalosporins in the mid-1980s, but could not pull it off. V-Guard has made indifferent progress with some of their new products. Without going into specifics, Shanghvi admitted to having made many mistakes: of not choosing certain new products as well as of having chosen some in the hope that they would grow. The main issue is not whether the choice of a product at its growth phase always leads to rapid growth, but whether the *chalnewala* item ever will. And to reduce the risks, one has to adopt elaborate processes rather than relying on one's hunches. Sathish Reddy of Dr Reddy's said that for too long the company had depended on the uncanny knack of Dr Anji Reddy to spot the winners (high-growth products) and to ensure that the company made and sold them right, and that he had instituted an elaborate process for new product search. Sun too has an elaborate process for new products introduction. Thus one may create organisational mechanisms for ensuring that there is adequate market, as also techno-commercial and process knowledge for a large enough number of products so that the total product portfolio always has one or two at the growth phase in the PLC. Only through entailing costs of such a process of information search may one reduce the risk of failure.

Marketing Mix and Competing in the Market

I am perhaps on a sticky wicket here. The field of marketing (other than that of HRD of course) is perhaps most polluted with general inanities passing off as great insights. I certainly wish to avoid inanities, and instead identify specific features of the marketing strategy adopted by the companies, that, to my mind, led to their success. And then draw generalisable lessons from their experiences. And when you have 10 companies in eight product markets, these generalisations can become a shade too general. Nevertheless, let us begin with how each of the sample companies formulated its marketing mix and attempted to compete.

Sun

Sun marketed speciality medicines, particularly those required in long-term therapy. As opposed to general purpose ethical medicines, which are recommended by a large number of general practitioners, speciality medicines are recommended by a smaller set of specialists. They, more or less conclusively, influence the actual buyer behaviour of the patients. Also, once a patient starts on one medicine, he will seldom change it except when the nature of the malady changes. Sun's marketing strategy revolved around this realisation and was hence based on making *first the company and then the product wanted* by the specialists. Its products and packaging are not particularly special or different. Nor has it ever made much noise about its price being low, affordable, etc., as have some other pharma companies. Its distribution system too has followed rather than led industry practice. The unique style of promotion through CME, through thoughtfully designed gifts (in the form of copies of current editions of journals/books or monograms on highly complex and professionally exciting topics), through developing an image of a scientifically oriented company and offering the Sunscan service to medical researchers, distinguish Sun's marketing and have been crucial to the company's success, giving it a unique image in the minds of the doctors. As one of its executive stated, the doctors started 'looking forward to the visit of our salesman to see what new information or paper he would bring rather than our salesmen having to wait for the doctors to give them time'. Thus it is to a very special and innovative manner of promotion, subtle and generalised to the level of the company rather than blunt and product specific, that the initial success of Sun must be credited.

Dr Reddy's Laboratories

For many years, DRL products were primarily bulk drugs. The company picked up and made those products that were till then imported, were outside the purview of DPCO and needed for treatment of commonly occurring maladies. By innovating on manufacturing processes enough to get protection under the Indian Patents Act and by offering the drug at prices much lower than that of the imported ones—in fact low enough for the formulators using the product for their medicines to be able to expand the market—the company was able to grow rapidly. In its formulations marketing, the company has striven to create an image of solid reliability. Thus image building rather than low pricing was its strategy in formulations, *but low pricing (as compared to the import option)* for high eventual volumes was the market strategy in the bulk-drugs segment.

Biocon

The company was at pains to explain to me that they added 'people and relations' as the fifth *P* to their marketing strategy. Its products—enzymes—are technical and their applications have to be custom made. The company did not stress the price or distribution strategies as the cause for its growth, but technical product-applications development and staying with the customer as being the central tenets of its marketing strategy. Building this image as a reliable company able to give highly competent technical support helped it grow. The technical (applications development) support is thus almost a feature of its products!

Orchid

The company has till date stuck to selling bulk drugs. Highly reliable and trustworthy product quality and building relationships with customers appear to be the major features of the marketing strategy of the company. And in a high-volume commodity such as cephalosporins, *price has to be competitive* vis-à-vis that of the European suppliers.

Mastek

The company has maintained a *high customer orientation* in its marketing strategy. They *even accepted penalty clauses for missing deadlines*. This customer orientation began with their initial customised applications software line and continued even in the small-value canned packages such as FINAC and STRAC. 'Though priced at about Rs 10,000, FINAC required a lot of servicing, ranging from telling the customer that he had not switched on the printer to helping him make specific applications using the package. Today, no one from Microsoft comes on a visit if you are unable to use Windows effectively. But our customers expected support and we thought that in the Indian circumstances of the mid-1980s it was necessary. However it was no longer viable for us by the 1990s. So we dropped FINAC.' This is how one Mastek executive explained this customer orientation. They dumped products from their portfolio (such as the accounting package) rather than ignore customer service. Thus instead of pricing or promotion, *post-purchase support* became the main plank of their marketing strategy. The later strategy of creating local subsidiaries in several countries rather than relying on project management with a temporary team also reflects the same concern.

Praj

In a sense, the company changed the definition of the product. This it did by incorporating championing of its customers' distillery projects at various levels of the bureaucratic maze in its marketing strategy. This was the most visible sign of its strategy, but at a more subtle level, it focused on improving the quality and performance of the equipment. The company conducted several seminars for educating the users and also engaged in applications engineering for various related systems. These highly focused, consistent and technically sound efforts were to give an added impetus to its marketing strategy. The *superior product features as compared to the traditional distillery* designs was of course a factor in its favour. The pricing of its product was bound to be favourable as compared to that of the multinational competitor which operated with massive overheads.

Sudha

Sudha has remained firmly in the commodity trading paradigm till now and cannot claim marketing excellence as a reason for its success.

Sumangal

Sumangal Prakashan introduced a *new product* (an almanac-cum-calendar) and distributed it very well, through two different channels—bookshops and newspaper agents. Subsequently, advertisement and promotion activities were undertaken on a large scale so that *Kalnirnaya* became almost a generic name for an almanac-cum-calendar. A household name. The promotion too was special, attempting to create a place for the product in the lives of ordinary folks, that a complete marathi household must have *Kalnirnaya* on its walls. *Bhintivari kalnirnaya asawe* was their most popular jingle. The focus is clearly on the middle-class urban Maharashtrian population. The promotion activities, including the use of back pages, etc., reflect this clear focus on offering a *cultural product*, not merely a calendar.

V-Guard

This marketer of voltage stabilisers offered a product for which the demand was a derived one. The company used the owner's personal contacts to place its stabilisers in those shops and establishments that sold refrigerators, televisions, etc., thus ensuring that the product was available at the same shop where the customer bought the appliance. The decision to price the product ten rupees more than that of the leading competitors communicated the hidden message of *superior quality and features*. This combination of ensuring that the product features and quality were consistently good and that the product was easily available in South India ensured growth.

Ashima

Ashima Syntex supplies lengths of denim and other textile fabric to garment manufacturers. Its approach was to focus on selling an industrial intermediary on *grounds of consistent quality, delivery schedules and price*, rather than resorting to brand equity. Its foray in consumer brands of readymades or ready-to-stitch products is recent and seems to follow conventional, me-too style marketing. Thus this company did not achieve growth because of a spectacular marketing strategy, but because of efficient administration of manufacturing processes which allowed it to take a low price–high volume position.

The above discussion is summed up in Table 4.1.

TABLE 4.1
Summary of Marketing Strategies of Successful Companies

Name	Plc	Prod	Place	Price	Prom	Rem
Sun	G	–	–	–	**	
DRL	G	–	–	**	–	
Orchid	S	**	–	**	–	
Biocon	S/G	**	–	–	–	TS
Mastek	G	*	**	–	–	TS
Sudha	S	–	–	**	–	
V-Guard	G	**	***	–	–	
S'mgl	G	**	**	***	***	Cult
Praj	G	*	–	–	***	TS
Ashima	G	*	–	**	–	

Note: The company names have been entered in cryptic form. A star in a cell indicates that the concerned company emphasised/used that element of the marketing mix with a view to fight the competition. The number of stars indicate our judgement of how strong was that emphasis. TS means that the company relied on technical support in applications development of its products as an element of marketing mix.

It emerges that four features of marketing mix have been used in prominence over others in competing in the market. These are:

- product features
- price as strategy (value for money)
- special type of promotion rather than advertising (bad news for the ad man)
- after-sales support as a means of establishing reputation

Product Features

The best way to compete in the long run is by offering a very good product. Thus by offering a good product and by continuously upgrading such attributes as deemed relevant by the buyer, one creates an invincible competitive advantage. This was realised by most of these companies. We thus find that

- Orchid established a good position in the international market for cephalosporins because of the superior quality of its products. It was not the first manufacturer of the drug, not even in India. Yet in less than three years, it achieved the reputation of being able to supply a very high and consistent quality drug. So much so that most competitors, even the older ones, started benchmarking their product *against* Orchid's. Not content with this, Orchid continues making visits to formulators in far-off China and other regions to constantly monitor the use conditions for the drug and modify the relevant parameters wherever appropriate.
- Biocon's enzymes are considered very good in quality and it is willing to work with the users to develop a product that meets their requirement.
- Sumangal designed a product that took the fancy of the urban Maharashtrian middle-class family, that held on to its cultural moorings despite the fast-paced city life. It continued to make product modifications (such as putting literary pieces on the reverse of the calendar) thus adding value of the desired kind to the product.
- V-Guard offered a voltage stabiliser with a built-in low-high cut-off feature, not common till then, and priced it slightly higher than the prevailing products. Consistently, it controlled the quality of its stabilisers so that in the whole of South India, it stands as a benchmark of stabiliser quality.

Price

When I argue that price was used as a weapon to win market share, I do not mean that the concerned company went in for a price war. Rather, it positioned itself against a competitor whose product was bound to be viewed as much more expensive. Thus:

- DRL came up with products—bulk drugs such as Sulphamethaxazole or Methyldopa—that were till then imported. When one looks at the tariff structure, the difficulty in getting foreign exchange allocation and the import license (I am talking of the bad old pre-liberalisation days), the net price of a DRL bulk drug was bound to be cheaper. The second element of DRL's strategy was to eventually cause a massive expansion of the market for the concerned medicine so that the company could sell more of its bulk drug, enabling it to exploit the available economies of scale. This strategy worked well till all the little fellows in India also started making the same bulk drug using their own technology (often bought from the market at the cost of a year's salary of the production manager!) and used even lower prices to compete with DRL.
- Sumangal had a peculiar problem when it started: people were used to getting the product for free. When the company started talking about selling a calendar, people thought it was being funny. Sumangal had to keep the prices low to encourage people to buy. A low price then became a necessary part of its marketing mix, and hence it had to expand volumes, which it did. Last year, they sold nearly five million calendars in Marathi alone, reaching almost every second Maharashtrian household!
- Industrial intermediate product makers have no choice but to use price positions to continuously win orders. They do not have to undercut, but offer the best quality at a low enough price which makes them the preferred

vendors. This is what Sudha, Orchid and Ashima had to do. Each then expanded the volume, reinforcing its ability to maintain a low-price position through economies of scale.

Special Type of Promotion Rather than Advertising

Barring Sumangal, which is in almost an FMCG line, virtually no other company spent much money on advertising. Whatever advertising they did was the corporate image type (such as Mastek's advertisement inviting the corporate gods to bestow free creativity in the company).

But the companies did undertake promotion and that too in a very special way. Sun sold itself as a company having high concern for professional excellence, as wishing to bring in the latest and the best in therapy to practice. They caught the prospective specialists young by donating expensive books to libraries of medical colleges, so that, as one executive claimed, several times the examination questions would be based on 'Sun's' books (that is, books donated by them). They were perhaps the first to start the CME programmes on private initiative. And to cap it all, they started the Sunscan service for helping researchers and students to access current literature. This is truly a unique form of promotion in a field where expensive gifts, sponsorships of trips abroad and liquor-and-dinner dominate.

Praj's initial efforts were even more remarkable. They discovered that setting up molasses-based distilleries involved, for cooperatives as well as private companies, such an arduous clearance procedure that offering assistance there helped win an order. So they piloted the proposals of especially the cooperatives through the bureaucratic labyrinth. And this really worked. Thus the company, whose job was mainly to design, engineer and commission the distillery, went around obtaining clearances, getting approvals and financial sanctions on behalf of the clients!

Sumangal undertook both promotion and advertising for its calendar. V-Guard focused more on push factors, by placing the stabilisers in white goods shops and offering better dealer discounts.

Superior After-Sales Service

The common experience of buyers, whether institutional or individual, is that most marketers are keen on making the sale but generally wash their hands off the customers thereafter. They might make a trip in the first month after the sale and then reappear at the time of making you sign the annual maintenance contract (AMC) at the end of the warranty period. And since every one of them looks to higher margins in the AMC than in the first deal, one often feels like throwing them out. In this context, those who offer superior after-sales service are bound to enjoy a good reputation. Companies that succeed seem to realise this. Thus:

Biocon believes that apart from the four *Ps* of marketing, the fifth *P* of people, that is, continued good relations with the customers, is crucial. They spend a lot of time on the buyer's processing line helping him obtain the desired results from their enzyme and engage in problem solving with him.

Mastek had been servicing customers not only for their custom-made software but even for low-volume canned packages such as FINAC. Since servicing needed local presence, they opened branches in different cities. Eventually, servicing became too expensive, particularly after imported canned packages flooded the market. Hence, rather than discontinuing the servicing, they withdrew the packages. If I cannot serve, I will not serve: now that is a good motto if one is for long-term business.

Praj, being a project commissioning company, had of course to take substantial interest in post-sales support activities. But what is remarkable is that they took this opportunity to establish a laboratory for distilleries, which eventually became a DSIR-approved research centre. This degree of interest naturally results in a post-sales support of a superior kind, not just mechanical repairs and refitting, which I presume they did as well, but also technical and analytical support needed for problem solving.

Learning from Marketing Successes

In *How Not to Ruin Your Small Industry*, I had stated that marketing myopia (and astigmatism!) is among the chief blunders that SSI units commit. My subsequent discussions with many of them only lend further weight to this observation. Levitt, in 'Marketing Myopia', *Harvard Business Review*, 1956, described marketing myopia as the syndrome where the marketer focuses on his products and not on the mission it serves. Such a restricted focus is said to lead to complacence and a high chance of redundancy as other ways of meeting the mission develop. What we have in several Indian SSIs is a focus on just the product, but only the sort of product the entrepreneur's unit makes right now! This when they do not have inflexible machines dedicated to making only one specific thing. For any change in specifications, the time requirement and cost, they feel, sort of become unreasonable. Their message is clear: 'This is what I make, buy it if you want; for anything else you have to wait or go elsewhere.' This is what I call astigmatism. Also, SSI units are unwilling to invest in upgrading their product features or quality, or to extend good technical support post-sales.

Among our successful companies, at least two (Sun and Biocon) go out of their way to develop products that satisfy the market's felt needs. Most others take a strong proactive stance in this matter. Pre- and post-sales support is also a prominent feature of their marketing strategy. The lesson is clear: giving up marketing astigmatism helps in the long run. The other lesson distilled in the first section is that successful companies pick up products that were at the growth phase of their respective PLC.

5

Managing Money: Financial Strategies of the Successful Companies

Three of the eight blunders I identified with the management of an SSI are about financial management. These are (a) expanding fixed assets without providing for enough working capital, (b) speculating on borrowed money and (c) doing informal business. Aside from this, management of working capital is critical to an SSI. The three features of managing finances in successful companies I am concerned with are first and foremost, the choice of capital structure, mix of equity and debt—whether short term or long term. Second comes the sourcing of capital: formal banking or institutional channels, IPO, euro-issues, etc. And finally, I would like to figure out the dominant method of managing working capital followed by these companies.

While this is not a text in financial management, a few terms need to be defined for the reader to interpret. Operating leverage indicates the fixed-cost intensity of a manufacturing unit and is defined as the ratio of incremental change in operating profit caused by a small change in sales. Usually, the higher the fixed costs as a proportion of sales, the higher the operating leverage. Financial leverage indicates the 'debt dependence' and is defined as the ratio of incremental change in net profit caused by a small change in operating profit. Usually, the higher the debt and hence interest costs, the higher the financial leverage. Finally, total leverage measures the total risk caused by both these factors and is measured as the ratio of the incremental change in net profit caused by a small change in sales. These values were calculated by using the financial figures of the companies and superimposing a small hypothetical variation in sales.

Sun

Capital Structure

Sun started with a small capital base of about Rs 1 lakh and formal loans from banks, etc., of about Rs 10 lakh. These included personal loans of about Rs 6 lakh taken by the chief promoter Shanghvi. The loans were largely unsecured, obtained by way of personal relations. The company systematically reinvested operational surpluses, so that by the time it became a public limited company, its equity base was about Rs 6 crore! By then it had taken formal institutional finance twice, once Rs 60 lakh in 1988 and then Rs 300 lakh in 1990. Even then, the debt–equity ratio was conservative—1.3 debt for 1 equity in 1994. By this time, personal loans were no longer needed. After 1994, due to its IPO at a very high premium, the company is cash surplus and there was some talk of negative interest cost!

	1990	1991	1992	1993	1994	1995	1996
Operating Leverage	1.13	1.24	1.03	1.04	1.04	1.05	1.00
Financial Leverage	1.12	1.13	1.17	1.35	1.16	1.00	1.00
Total Leverage	1.26	1.40	1.21	1.42	1.20	1.05	1.00

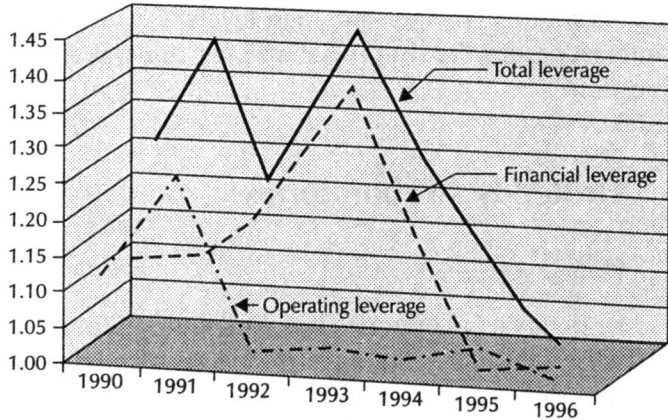

Sourcing and Use of Funds

Till 1994, the funds used were either internal accruals or formal loans, the first and the only IPO occurring in 1994. Funds were deployed till 1990 almost evenly between fixed and current assets. By 1993, fixed assets soaked up Rs 639 lakh as compared to a working capital of Rs 882 lakh. As of the last reported figures, the capital fund of Rs 169 crore (15 crore equity, 113 retained surpluses, 18 in loans and some Rs 24 crore in current liabilities) were applied thus: Rs 53 crore in fixed assets and the balance in current assets. Thus the company has consistently ensured that its working capital needs do not suffer for want of funds.

Managing Working Capital

Between 1993 and 1996, years for which the data is available, inventories varied between 1.7 to 2 months of sales, rising in the last year. Debtors remained consistently around 2 months of sales, reducing marginally towards the last year. Clearly, the company used high inventories and longer credit periods as ways of securing higher sales. This was facilitated by relatively high margins on products (consistently over 100 per cent on materials consumed) and prudently designed capital structure. Thus despite high levels of working capital, interest costs were simply not a worry, nor was liquidity in question.

Dr Reddy's Laboratories

Capital Structure

Dr Reddy's Laboratories was Anji Reddy's fourth venture, following Uniloids, Standard Organics, and a finance and leasing company. So it is necessary to look at the history of financial policies he followed. Uniloids was floated with the equity of some five lakh rupees and loans from a financial institution. Standard Organics was jointly owned by Anji Reddy and C.C. Reddy with some debts again. The lease and finance company was used primarily as an instrument for collecting public funds, which were presumably invested in the two ventures DRL and Cheminor. DRL itself started with a total investment of Rs 120 lakh of which Rs 50 lakh came from promoters and the balance as loans from AP financial corporations. Dr Reddy's Laboratories made an IPO of convertible debentures in 1985 and a GDR issue in 1994. Its debt–equity ratio in 1985 was 4 debt for 1 equity, but that was pending allocation of converted shares against the convertible portion of CD. The debt–equity ratios of 1.79 debt to 1 equity in 1986 and 2.04 to 1 in 1987 came down sharply thereafter as surpluses were retained and ploughed back and as IPOs occurred at a premium to domestic prices. Thus to begin with, financing was risky but it became conservative after the gamble paid off.

	1993	1994	1995	1996	1997
Operating Leverage	1.09	1.05	1.08	1.07	1.13
Financial Leverage	1.20	1.17	1.08	1.11	1.24
Total Leverage	1.30	1.23	1.16	1.19	1.41

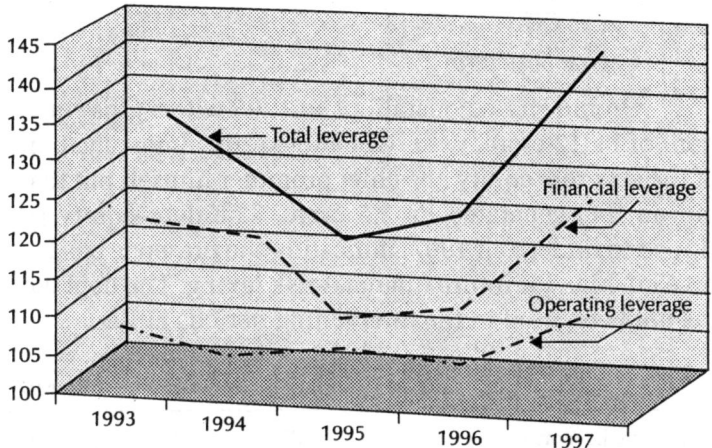

Sourcing and Use of Funds

After 1986, funds obtained either from promoters and investors or from institutions were invested in fixed and current assets in the proportion of almost 1:2. Thus the company did not expand its fixed asset base rapidly. The major expansions occurred in 1987 when the Quinolones factory was expanded and in 1991 when the Foundation was set up. Thereafter the company has had a fixed investment of a few crores each year in incremental additions.

Managing Working Capital

The company had current assets worth almost six months' sales in 1985. This number remained around five months except in 1992 when it was under four months (but it shot up to over six months the next year, mainly due to DRL's decision to start selling formulations. Thus like so many companies aiming for volumes in their goods, DRL opted for a high working capital strategy, as it happens, after the financial leverage was brought down substantially.

Orchid

Capital Structure

Orchid started operations in 1993 with a gross investment of Rs 12 crore, with debt and equity almost matching. Of the six crore equity, the chief promoter himself put in two and an IPO generated Rs 2.5 crore. The debt–equity ratio dipped to under 1 in 1997, indicating the presence of a fairly large cushion for future financial risk taking. The debt mode has not been used in the intervening periods either.

	Mar.94	Mar.95	Mar.96	Mar.97
Operating Leverage	1.07	1.07	1.07	1.09
Financial Leverage	1.29	1.23	1.24	1.25
Total Leverage	1.38	1.32	1.33	1.36

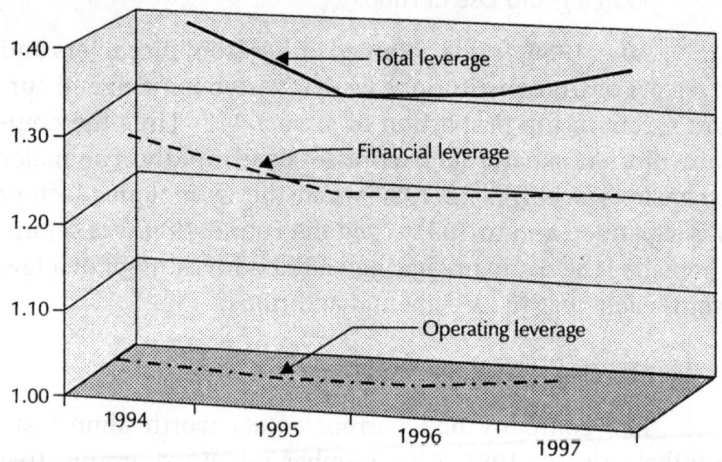

Application of Funds

In 1994, as compared to Rs 12 crore invested in net fixed assets, the current assets were worth Rs 10.3 crore. The proportion between fixed and current assets changed in favour of fixed assets in 1997, the fixed assets at Rs 145.6

crore far exceeding the Rs 85.8 crore worth of current assets. The company is clearly building up its production and research abilities in preference to creating distribution and trade logistics.

Managing Working Capital

Being a 100 per cent EOU, the company has an advantage in that much of its business is against irrevocable Letters of Credit. The inventories have remained below three months' sales despite massive jumps in sales volumes. Debtors have actually shrunk from a high of almost five months' sales in 1995 to less than a month in 1997, despite high rates of growth. What one sees then is a company conservative in financing, investing at a high rate in fixed assets and simultaneously controlling its working capital needs despite a growing business.

Mastek

Capital Structure

The company started in 1982 with a tiny capital base of only Rs 400. The contributed share capital remained at this level till 1990, when the reserves and assets built through retained earnings were capitalised at Rs 10 lakh and then raised through a bonus issue to Rs 20 lakh. TDICI then pumped in a venture capital of Rs 3 lakh. Just before its IPO in 1992, the shareholding was Rs 187 lakh with promoters (78 per cent) and Rs 52 lakh with TDICI (22 per cent). The IPO brought in Rs 60 lakh and reduced the holdings of promoters as well as TDICI. Till then, there was no debt at all. In 1994, 75 per cent of the total capital employed of Rs 15.1 crore came from own funds and balance from debt. This ratio of 1 debt to 3 equity remained at that level for the next two years. Thus here too, the company shows signs of conservatism.

	1994	1995	1996
Operating Leverage	1.17	1.28	1.35
Financial Leverage	1.19	1.26	1.57
Total Leverage	1.39	1.61	2.12

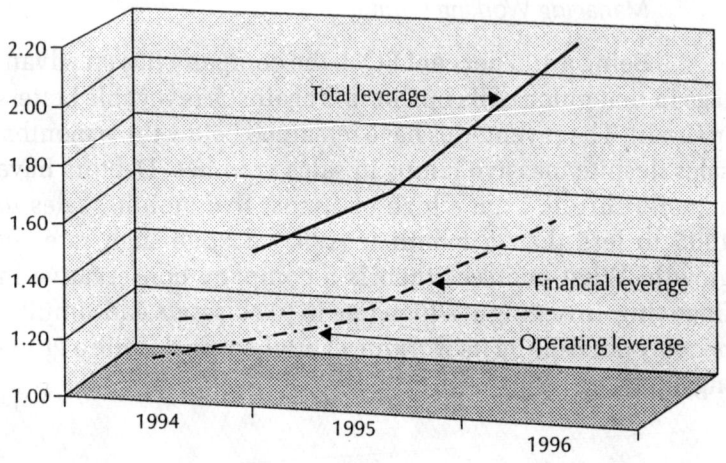

Sourcing of Funds

In 1994, of the total assets of Rs 15.1 crore, Rs 13.2 crore was in the form of current assets (87 per cent), almost Rs 5.9 crore in cash and bank balances, and the balance as sundry debtors and advances. For a software business, inventories are irrelevant but such huge bank balances seem strange. The proportion of current assets came down a bit to about 67 per cent in 1996. Sundry debtors contributed the largest chunk to current assets in that year. Most of the funds deployed in these assets came from retained earnings. The surpluses contributed Rs 13.2 crore as compared to debts of under Rs 5 crore. Thus the company is ploughing its retained earnings to finance its increasing working capital needs. The latter is ever expanding because Mastek subsidiaries abroad need operational bridging finance for seeding, winning and completing business. Since they are neither capitalised adequately in the host country nor have sufficient fixed assets there, they cannot hope to use local loans. Hence Mastek has to finance them in the form of advances or loans. This possibly explains the motivation for keeping large bank balances.

Sudha

Capital Structure

Sudha began with a project cost of Rs 110 lakh, of which promoters' equity contribution was Rs 53 lakh. The company borrowed Rs 50 lakh from financial institutions. The capital structure in 1992 was Rs 145 lakh of own funds to under Rs 50 lakh of debt. That year began the expansion programmes which needed borrowings. The debt–equity ratio changed from this conservative financing pattern to a much riskier pattern of Rs 11.6 crore in debt to Rs 3.4 crore in equity (a ratio of 3:1) in 1997. During this time, the company capitalised some of its reserves but did not choose to go in for an IPO. This preference to a debt rather than an IPO appears to have been caused by the depressed market conditions.

	1992	1993	1994	1995	1996
Operating Leverage	1.70	1.45	1.35	1.18	1.23
Financial Leverage	1.62	1.51	1.32	1.74	3.36
Total Leverage	2.75	2.18	1.79	2.05	4.14

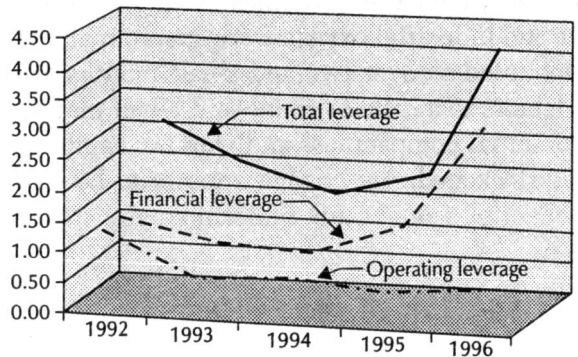

Sourcing and Use of Funds

The total change in capital employed was Rs 18.7 crore in the five-year period between 1992 and 1997, comprising Rs 2.5 crore through retained earnings, Rs 5.3 crore in current liabilities and Rs 10.5 crore in debts. This high-leveraged financing was deployed for building up the gross block by Rs 9.2 crore and current assets by Rs 9.5 crore. The total current assets of Rs 2.2 crore in 1992 comprised inventories (50 per cent) and sundry debtors (22 per cent). The current assets of Rs 13.6 crore comprised inventories of Rs 8.4 crore (over 60 per cent) and sundry debtors of Rs 4 crore (30 per cent). Since the company deals in a commodity of volatile price, it is taking a much larger risk in putting more in inventories. This is partly explained by the fact that the product mix has changed much in favour of industrial intermediaries such as fatty acid distillates. This increased level of risk in modes of financing as well as in modes of deploying funds perhaps explains why the company shies from an IPO.

Managing Working Capital

In 1992, sundry debtors amounted to less than half a month's sales while inventories amounted to a little over a month-and-a-half. In 1995, when the expansion process was in full swing, these numbers were about the same in both the cases. In 1997, after the new lines of fatty acid distillates, glycerine and industrial oxygen were operational, the inventories amounted to over two-and-a-half months' sales and sundry debtors to a little over one-and-a-half months. Thus while the initial compactness and working capital management has slackened, the change appears to be due to the enhancement of product mix rather than any slackening of discipline.

Praj

Capital Structure

Mr Chowdhary's first investment occurred in 1984 when he constructed a small shed in Bhosri. The shed employed six workers and did small engineering jobs. He invested around Rs 5 lakh in this venture, with small loans of about Rs 3 lakh for sustaining the business. He got the first order for a distillery plant in 1985, its value being Rs 81 lakh, but since the principal agreed to pay directly the bought-out components and materials worth Rs 50 lakh, Praj's financing needs were smaller. The expenses on other items were met out of the project funds released by the client. The next major need for money arose when a bank guarantee had to be furnished to the Austrian principal of fermentation technology. Praj was able to get this from Bank of Maharashtra.

Praj was the first SSI in the engineering sector to get the TDICI equity as a venture capital. In 1992, one year before the IPO, Praj had employed a total of Rs 4.49 crore of long-term resources, of which Rs 60 lakh came from subscribed share capital, Rs 3 crore from retained earnings and Rs 90 lakh from loans. By 1996, the capital employed had risen to Rs 24.1 crore, of which own funds accounted for Rs 17.5 crore. Thus, throughout, the company has kept its debt well below owned funds. However, current liabilities are always very high, some Rs 7.1 crore, or almost twice the long-term funds in 1992, and Rs 20.7 crore in 1996. This is caused and balanced by the need to maintain high current assets in the form of unfinished contracts as well as materials.

	1992	1993	1994	1995	1996
Operating Leverage	1.10	1.01	1.01	1.01	1.05
Financial Leverage	1.26	1.04	1.04	1.06	1.13
Total Leverage	1.39	1.05	1.06	1.08	1.19

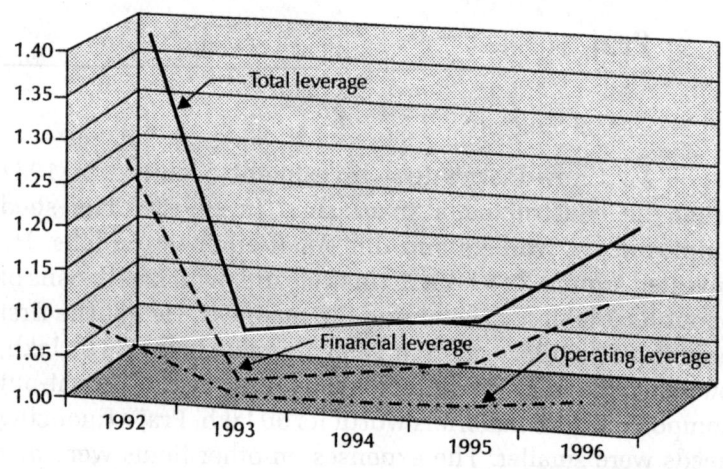

Use of Funds

Of the total asset base of Rs 8.9 crore in 1992, Rs 8.3 crore was in current assets. Such preponderance of current assets continued throughout, reduced albeit in 1996 when current assets were at Rs 34.5 crore in a total asset base of Rs 44.3 crore. Thus, while the fixed asset base increased from just Rs 60 lakh in 1992 to over Rs 8.2 crore in 1996, this was well short of the rise in long-term finance by over Rs 14.5 crore. Clearly, the company is prudently using long-term resources such as retained earnings to fund the current assets.

For Praj, the working capital management primarily involves matching the timing of procurement of materials and services with that of obtaining advances from the principals. Since this match can never be complete, the company has been doing the next best—using current liabilities to finance burgeoning current assets. Working capital, that is, net current assets were Rs 1.1 crore in 1992 and have become Rs 14.7 crore in 1996, indicating that the company has had to finance this rise through long-term finances.

Ashima Syntex

Capital Structure

Initially when Ashima was involved in texturising of Polyester Yarn, its capital structure was as per the industry norms. However after the shift to the denim and cotton textile business, the debt–equity ratio was brought down from 3:1 to 1.1:1. Equity has moved from Rs 5.44 crore in 94 to Rs 33.35 crore in 1995. Reserve and surpluses have increased by more than 11 times to Rs 177.39 crore. Cash and bank balance, with a three-fold increase, in 1996 shows around Rs 27 crore on account of the debenture application money.

	Jul.94	Jun.95	Jun.96	Jun.97
Operating Leverage	1.20	1.31	1.39	1.41
Financial Leverage	1.55	1.15	1.06	1.19
Total Leverage	1.87	1.52	1.48	1.67

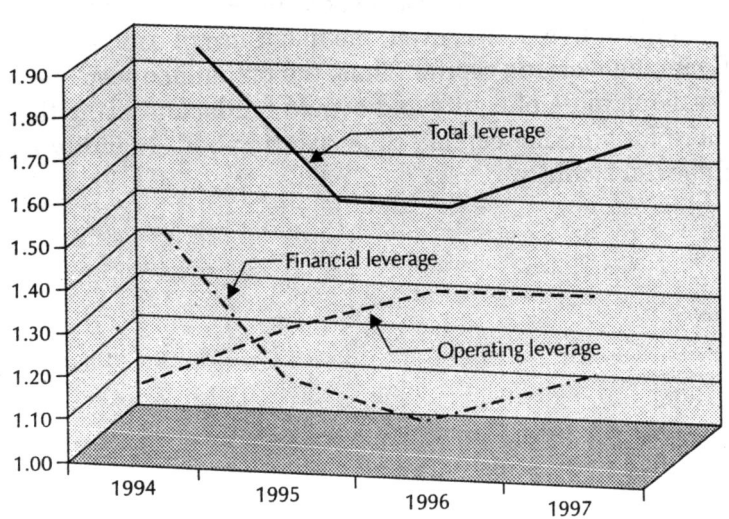

Managing Working Capital

At Ashima, each division head gives a monthly working capital projection. The corporate finance group, after interacting with the division heads, consolidates the group working capital requirement. The operational team closely monitors any deviation in the monthly limits and keeps the corporate finance informed about these. The company operates through the bank for its working capital requirements. The term loan and working capital facilities show an increase over the years (from Rs 11.40 crore in 1994 to 70.56 crore in 1996), although in the year 1997 it shows a slight fall to Rs 68.35 crore.

We do not have the financial information to comment on the financial strategy followed by Biocon, Sumangal and V-Guard. The features of financial management in the seven companies described above can be summarised in Table 5.1.

What I wish to emphasise is that in six of the seven companies, the debt–equity ratio was either smaller than one or at least was substantially brought down over a period of time. Clearly, each company seems to be conservatively managed. Second, in five of the seven, the major use of capital was in financing working capital. Thus, the preference seems to be for using more of equity and owned funds, and using them more for working capital, thus ensuring both liquidity and financial stability.

TABLE 5.1
Financial Management in Successful Companies

Sl. No.	Name	Capital Structure	Use of Funds	Mgmt. of W/C	Remark
1	Sun	D/E changed from 10 to 1.3	Used funds for CA	Steady, dictated by trade norm	Resists fresh public equity
2	DRL	D/E reduced from 4 to 1	Deployed more for CA	Aggressive, aiming at sales	The company has GDR
3	Orchid	D/E less than 1	Built FA	Very tight	Being an EOU helps
4	Mastek	D/E less than 1	Huge CA built	No comments	Overseas subsidiaries needed money
5	Praj	D/E less than 1	Huge CA	Driven by industry	Project business needs money, but it cannot borrow
6	Sudha	D/E rose from 1 to 3.	FA and CA built equally	Inventory and debtors rose.	Debts for expanding in non-traditional products
7	Ashima	D/E came down from 3:1 to 1.1:1	Built FA	Inventories and debtors rose	Invested on the building capacities

6

Manufacturing and Logistics in the Successful Companies

Success is 95 per cent...

As this expression suggests, brilliant strategising for dramatic success is as rare as being born in a royal family. Most entrepreneurs and companies have to work hard to achieve success and become medium-/large-scale enterprises. And nowhere is the effort more gruelling and more rewarding than in the management of logistics of manufacture, procurement, purchase, sales distribution, etc. It is gruelling because it is repetitive, unglamorous. Sometimes this requires efforts in difficult working conditions. Someone has to go through a given process in its full details, study each operation in its minutest detail and see how it can be modified so that just a little less material, labour, time, fuel, power, etc., would be consumed. And then repeat it ad infinitum. After all, reduction in net effort (represented by material or labour consumption per unit output) resulting from the learning curve (more generally, the experience curve) occurs precisely because workers and engineers cumulate such minor but cumulatively useful insights and knowledge about the process. As a successful entrepreneur of the 1980s said, 'I become like a worm moving around inside every section of my process. My head is full of details about the process and its steps. I think of nothing else but the process improvement. And then one by one things begin to become clear: heat this longer, let the material flow be changed such, reduce the storage time there... And then I have to work through the shop floor and the sullen staff to actually try these changes. Tiring process, but that is how we reduce cost and cycle time!' Incidentally, he patented one or two changes in this manner. He also got the manufacturers of his machines to incorporate some 36 changes in the machines. He redesigned most of the process flow to achieve unique low-cost positions.

At the initial stage of a small enterprise, it has virtually no solid competitive advantage. If it is 'expert', creative or inventive, yes it would have the advantage of its expertise or of being the first to start a product. But India has experts going dime a dozen, at least those specialising in learning from other companies and putting in practice in one's shop floor. Products get copied fast. Other almanac-cum-calendars followed *Kalnirnaya* in just a few years. Dr Reddy could exploit the new drug market profitably only for a few years. Others soon come up with me-too products capable of replacing the 'innovations'. Expertise and creativity are no longstanding advantages. Hence most of the firms have very little inherent competitive advantage.

Usually firms start by building this advantage in the market. But more pronouncedly perhaps, they do so by making a better and cheaper product. As is commonly understood, business firms tend to be centred around production activities in their initial stages. (The classical model of business growth follows the sequence of production-centred business, followed by finance-centred, followed by market-centred. By these terms we mean that the primary managerial attention is focused on these departments.) Thus it would be surprising if the successful firms did not pay attention to manufacturing and logistics at the growth stage. Nevertheless, what is crucial is making things better and cheaper and then selling them better and at lower costs.

The cases studied throw up the following messages about successful companies:

- They chose or developed technologies that were new, superior or even state of the art.
- Such companies attached significant importance to the manufacturing function as such and engaged in bootstrapping, that is, deriving significant improvements and benefits by arduous and systematic hard work in improving manufacturing and logistics.
- They matched asset expansion with sales growth.

Let us look at each of these issues in detail.

Technology Choice and Development

I am particularly interested here in looking at engineering and applications technology in logistics. There are many options available to an entrepreneur: following low-level technology, copying technology from wherever one can, developing on one's own, modifying existing technology, formally sourcing technology through collaboration agreement, etc. Second, the decision regarding technology may be just a one-time decision, a configuration to be chosen once and followed for all times to come, such as technology allegedly followed by a famous car manufacturer of the country (the one who makes brand new vintage cars!). Alternatively, technology-related decisions could and need to be taken continuously. The interesting question is whether entrepreneurs follow the same basic strand of decision preference throughout or changes their thinking over time. What did our successful companies do?

DRL

Anji Reddy's special aptitude in chemical process engineering and his experience as a member of the chief technologist's team helped the company to throughout develop its own new technology for making an established drug. The company deliberately followed a procedure of evolving a technology that would allow it to manufacture an established drug without violating Indian Patents Act as it stands. The manufacturing equipments, etc., have been fairly standard. It is the chemistry and the chemical process where such technological choice was involved. DRL thus relied on new technologies, new at least for this country, and this they did several times.

Biocon

The first manufacturing activity of Biocon was manufacture of isinglass and papaine. This followed what the entrepreneur called an 'uninspiringly low' technology. But to Biocon's credit, even at that stage, within a few years they hired extremely well-trained technocrats to develop their own technology and products through R&D. Thereafter, they have been at the forefront of fermentation technology. They became among the first contract R&D companies in the country. Clearly, developers and users of new technology, time and again.

Sudha

The choice of technology made by Sudha, whether for solvent extraction of RB or for physical or chemical refining, offers no special features. It is the 'operating technology' used in managing inward logistics which was superior. This distinguishing technology comprised linking up with suppliers of RB all over to expand the length of the processing calendar. Similarly, hydrogenation technology or fatty acid distillation technology adopted here was quite simple and routine. As an executive said, 'we take technical advice but most of the engineering work we like to do ourselves', and considering that all the three key executives were non-technical persons, this only reflects on the basic simplicity of the technology. Thus the basic processing technology was an established one. Their subsequent choice reflects time and again the preference for the old and the established. But the logistics were managed better, showing new operating technology.

Orchid

The company chose the then state-of-the-art technology to make cephalosporins from Pen G. Subsequently the company has been adding technological components for backward integration as well as for effluent treatment. In so far as sterile products are concerned, the company insisted upon a complex, expensive and current technology for product manufacturing as well as for air handling. It has the best ETP known in the country and has become the only zero-effluent company in the region. Thus the company has a strong orientation towards hitech, demonstrating its choice for superior technology.

Ashima

Ashima has laid great stress on commissioning the best technology available worldwide. The experience of the polyester business and the traditional textile mills taught Ashima two lessons—to source a capital-intensive technology and second, to have the scale of manufacturing operation so large as to create an entry barrier for the small players. Technology is being chosen keeping in mind the international parameters for quality. It has been sourced from Japan, Germany, Switzerland, the UK and even India. In 1993, when the Tsudakoma airjet weaving facility was installed to manufacture the gray fabric, it was the first of its kind in

India. Thus the company's preference for superior technology is clearly demonstrated. Whereas the basic technology in the textile industry has remained stable, the changes have occurred in the area of speed and quality of output. The chairman and the executive director constantly scan through textile equipment journals in order to keep track of the technological changes. A clear preference for new and superior technology seems to be a recurring pattern here.

Praj

Praj took the initiative to adopt a technology till then not seen in the country. Majority of Indian distilleries had adopted batch-type fermentation technology. Praj tied up with an Austrian firm Vogelbusch and offered continuous-type fermentation equipment for alcohol making. By further working on this, they developed fermentation technology for feedstock other than molasses, such as sorghum. Later, by tying up with foreign collaborators, Praj tried to bring in technologies in brewing, thermal engineering, centrifuging and air dispersion drying. Thus Praj has tried to choose technologies that were different from the ones available within the country and that offered scope for indigenisation over time. Here too the pattern is recurrent.

In the case of Mastek, the question of technology for manufacturing or logistics does not present itself in the same manner. In terms of software and pertinent hardware support, the company certainly was at the forefront of developments in its field of activities (namely, applications software for business). Sumangal has followed a rather conventional production technology. In fact, it used to get its printing done on job-work basis and did not have any printing facility till 1979. Then it acquired a fairly ordinary machine for printing calendars. It acquired high-quality machines much later, around 1987, and then it had to take printing job work from outside. Thus in this sense, Sumangal too allowed its fixed assets base to follow rather than lead sales growth. V-Guard's technology basically involved assembly of electronic components for making its stabilisers, and this it did in its factory for a while. But when labour trouble came, the company wound it up and went in for subcontracted manufacture.

Matching Productive Asset Expansion with Sales Growth

Clearly, at the time of establishment of factories and fixed assets of that kind, most firms would have larger capacities than warranted by actual sales. I generalise on the factory and use the word *assets* or *productive assets*. As sales grow, assets might start falling short of capacities and need to be expanded to keep pace with sales. There are some basic options available to firms for matching asset expansion with sales growth—getting work done on job-work basis from outsiders, making incremental additions to assets, duplicating existing facilities without technological upgradation, creating brand new facilities with upgraded technology and lastly, buying/acquiring others' facilities. These options are valid for companies whose product line has remained relatively stable. In case during the first phase, the product line itself has got changed or if there has been a move for forward or backward integration, then this set would not apply, as new facilities would have to be put up. Let us see how successful companies expanded assets to keep pace with sales, which option they followed and whether there is a pattern.

Sun

When Sun started operations from Gujarat, it already had an established market for its products in the East, by getting their products manufactured in third-party premises. They started it in Gujarat by creating a factory to meet own needs. The first factory was in a tiny *gala* in GIDC Vapi estate. It was an unassuming little factory. Sun's original unit in Vapi built in 1982 had to be expanded almost immediately to house the quality control department. The company expanded the facilities twice before 1985, as the sales grew quickly. This expansion was done in an incremental manner—adding a blender here, a grinder there and a packaging line somewhere in between. Then came a sister company—Unimed—managed by Sun. This was a full-blown factory at Halol. Sun's own expansions seem to have followed and not led, sales growth. Till well into the 1990s, Sun relied on several third-party manufacturing contracts to augment its own production facilities for meeting the sales targets. This picture continues throughout. In its later life, Sun set up a bulk drug unit at Panoli and a formulations unit at Silvassa. Sun acquired facilities of the companies in which it took a controlling interest and bought a plant from an MNC. Sun does not give the image of a manufacturing-dominated organisation wherein marketing has to run overtime to ensure capacity utilisation. It works the other way round. Its approach in choosing a mode is pragmatic (making the best use of available resources) rather than absolute (pitting for the technologically most-sophisticated option).

DRL

For expanding its market in India, the company followed a strategy of manufacturing an established but imported drug and making it available at reduced prices. The size of its manufacturing facilities at the start of each new product has more often than not been larger than the concerned product's sales. This seems to have been followed consistently. Later on, it bought up or acquired formulations units in order to establish a foothold in that market. DRL did not go through elaborate phases of massive expansion of facilities. This is because bulk-drug manufacture basically needs reaction vessels, utilities such as vacuum, steam and air-handling, etc. The same basic hardware (with possible additions at the margin) can handle different products. Its expansions came in the 1990s when the company had grown quite big. Thus it followed the option of buying facilities for formulations, making incremental additions and then setting up a whole new factory, in that order.

Biocon

Till 1997, Biocon's manufacturing facilities were small in size. Partly, the size of the enzyme markets itself was small. But more importantly, the entrepreneur never wanted to get into any 'commodity-like business, where large volumes hold the key to profits'. Only when it formed Helix, a speciality antibiotic company, that the size of the manufacturing facility became possibly larger. The company went through more phases of diversification rather than expansion projects. From Biocon, it first formed Biocheminzyme for researching and developing the process of fermentation for making enzymes as its first project. It was a natural extension of the R&D activities started by the company four years after it commenced production. Biocon Quest (BQ) was the only expansion project which took the work of Biocheminzyme to scale in terms of manufacturing quantities. A 100 per cent export-oriented project, BQ made enzymes. Syngene was a contract research company. These projects came between 1989 and 1997, or not before some eight years after the first company was formed. Here too, assets followed rather than led sales growth. Thus there was a combination of incremental addition of assets and new equipment for the changed line.

Mastek

For Mastek, matters pertaining to logistics cannot be discussed in the same manner as for the above companies. The company has not been in manufacturing at all. The choice of technology must be looked at differently. To begin with, Mastek did not have any hardware technology per se but would develop applications software on whatever computer the clients had. When it came to making and selling products such as FINAC, Mastek resolved to base its technology on whatever was the most popular desktop in the market, as it had to install its products on customers' computers. In terms of its own hardware, Mastek had been slow and careful to invest, building infrastructure in phases rather than at one go. 'In our earlier offices, the number of chairs were often less than the number of persons employed as many would be out in the field. And so when all came in at the same time, someone had to remain standing', said one company executive, remembering the situation in the late 1980s. 'Even the SEEPZ facility was made ready in phases', according to the management. Only by the 1990s, almost after a decade, the company expanded its hardware. One must remember that Mastek's expansion is more in terms of setting up and supporting subsidiary companies floated in a number of host countries. Since these had low capital to begin with and no assets which had collateral value, they found it difficult to get loans in the host country and hence Mastek had to support them regularly. This expansion occurred very quickly indeed. Between 1990 and 1997 the company had subsidiaries in four countries.

Orchid

Since the company decided to focus only on bulk drugs and since it catered to a huge market in China, East Asia and some other unregulated countries, its manufacturing facilities have been large and capital intensive. Its business is what Biocon described as 'huge, commodity-like business where volumes hold the key to profits'. The company expanded rapidly. In the three years between 1994 (the first full year of commercial operations) and 1997, there were two expansions and a third was being planned! This company seems to be putting up new facilities with state-of-the-art technology, after one phase of expansion.

Sudha

Sudha has been conservative. Its solvent extraction plant at 150 TPD was of a modest size in the rice-growing region of East Godawari. The refining capacity first put up was for only a portion of the RB oil produced and then too for only partial refining. Hydrogenation facility too was for only 'industrial hydrogenation'. The refining capacity had to be expanded. Thus till 1992, or for almost a dozen years after start, the company expanded slowly, in phases. It was only post-1994 that the pace of expansion quickened. The asset expansion was of incremental addition-type for refining or hydrogenation. Later it was in the nature of vertical integration. Hence new facilities were added.

Sumangal

The company's printing facilities were added between 1985 and 1995 in a phased manner. Since its own production was intensely seasonal, it deferred investment in printing facilities till either it was sure of getting enough job work in its off-season and till its own volumes justified expansion. Thus Sumangal's manufacturing base followed the sales growth.

V-Guard

The company began as a backyard manufacturer of stabilisers, acquired a formal factory set-up and then disbanded it in favour of subcontracted manufacture. Asset expansion was thus not an issue. This could be linear with sales since it was always possible to contract out volumes at the rate at which sales growth occurred.

Ashima

Ashima added denim, spin fabric, yarn-dyed and knitwear facilities in quick succession. The capacities were added keeping in view the global and domestic market demand. They are all located at the 'Texellence Complex' in Ahmedabad where they share common utilities. Thus both vertical integration and adding new machinery for a different range of products happened. Each time, the options taken appear to be more absolutist, wishing to have state-of-the-art technology and taking pride in it.

Praj

Praj is a project engineering firm and not a manufacturer by itself. As such it did not have much manufacturing till 1992, or some seven years after start. In 1992 it started manufacture of heat exchangers but there was not much further expansion in manufacturing. Capabilities to absorb technologies, develop new processes and implement projects using these new technologies and processes were acquired, but manufacturing remained small.

Bootstrapping

By 'bootstrapping' I mean deriving significant improvements and benefits by arduous and systematic hard work in improving manufacturing and logistics. A company looks at every element of the logistics carefully for identifying and adopting ways of improving it. Every step is taken for superior quality or efficiency (in terms of material or utility usage and cycle time). Modifications are tried and implemented before attention shifts to the next element. Thus bootstrapping is a long-drawn process. That is what later gets summed up under experience curves. As to which part of the total process should a company apply its mind and engage in bootstrapping would perhaps depend on its own perception of business. And also where it sees the highest marginal returns to efforts. Thus if hypothetically, the highest marginal returns are in sound purchasing of the raw material, that is where attention will be focused. If distribution offers such rewards, that is where it will focus.

Since my colleagues and I studied these companies in 1997, we could only learn what the companies chose to tell us. None of us witnessed the process of growth per se, but only heard retrospective commentaries about them. I have mentioned the bootstrapping efforts emphatically whenever we were told about them. It is possible, in fact more than likely, that such efforts were on even for other companies in this sample, but have not been narrated for some collateral reason (e.g., it may not have appeared pertinent to the researcher or to the executives being interviewed, etc.). Such absence of emphasis definitely suggests reduced importance to that activity in that company.

Sun

Sun competed well not on account of low-cost positions but superb market creation and nurturing efforts. As such, its efforts on bootstrapping were never particularly stressed by executives I talked to. Relatively speaking, these efforts were more pronounced in case of logistics of purchase of materials (including active medicaments for psychotropic drugs). Bootstrapping was attempted in distribution logistics as well. A senior manager said that identifying the best sources of active medicament was clearly a competitive strength of Sun. The importance of distribution logistics became more pronounced as this activity had to cope with several *sources* of medicines in the Sun fold, including third-party factories, and hundreds of 'sinks' or destinations (C&F depots, etc.). This happened particularly after there was a trauma connected with some sales tax documentation due to a system that had started cracking up under extra load.

DRL

DRL does not provide enough evidence of bootstrapping. This is not to say that there were no efforts in this direction at DRL, but the executives we met did not expand on this theme. They did talk of the company's knack in identifying products that could be made without violating the Patents' Act, that were till then imported and hence offered a price advantage to DRL, that were outside DPCO, etc. They also spoke of the strategy of expanding the domestic market for the product as well as capturing new markets in unregulated countries, but processing efficiency was not stressed. The importance of continued process development research to sort out problems encountered during manufacturing was mentioned and this was the farthest they went. The company valued R&D as well as process development. But manufacturing per se did not seem to get as large an importance within the company. The efforts focused at improving process efficiency got under way once the company's growth pace based on Quinlones started losing steam due to increased competition.

Orchid

These efforts were reported emphatically as being central to the scheme of things. Constant attention to process parameters, to the chemistry involved and to supply of utilities has been responsible for efficient and high-quality manufacture. Elaborate reporting as well as management control procedures reflect the company's emphasis on process improvement. Orchid maintains process development laboratories aside from and outside the R&D laboratory, which is a separate set-up. Manufacturing, utilities, logistics of handling both imported and export cargo, and water supply for manufacturing operations and effluent treatment have all been regarded as being very important. The company has a small marketing set-up which takes care of commercial operations of exports and the legal aspects involved in medicines market. Within the company, finance and manufacturing assume great importance. Orchid is certainly a manufacturing-driven company.

Sudha

Efforts to achieve high technical efficiency have been consistent and have borne fruit. This was demonstrated in:

- ensuring high capacity utilisation (something like 270 days of operation of the SE plant, probably one of the highest in the country, the industry average being around 180–200)
- defining process parameters that compare well with industry averages
- developing a scheme of proper utilisation of RB of different grades
- keeping a range of back-up utilities needed

The company has been able to achieve commendable efficiencies. Since it focuses on manufacturing margins and not trading margins (this is abundantly evidenced by its decision to let out facilities on contract work during export boom) it attaches high importance to efficiency in this activity. This emphasis is quite uncommon in an industry dominated by trader-like mindset and preoccupation with export trade-related matters.

V-Guard

These efforts were continuous, designs were looked at, as was product quality. The company evolved a subcontracted system of manufacturing with tight quality control. That is its strength in this field. Maintaining high quality subcontracted manufacture for which components are supplied from the focal unit definitely needs well thought-out logistics. The company has been able to develop these.

Ashima

Ashima has sourced the basic RM (dyes, etc.) from the recommended sources. It has also laid stress on adherence to manufacturer-recommended maintenance parameters. At times the company has paid high premium for the imported materials over the local products only because that was recommended by the equipment manufacturer. The Executive Director (Technical) was proud of the fact that 'After observing the performance of machines at Ashima, the suppliers are ready to come down to our price level in order to get repeat orders.' The company has emphasised on the manufacturing process and the quality of output. Chief operating officers are responsible for the manufacturing. Over a period of time, due to this strict adherence to good manufacturing practices, it has achieved cost advantages.

Praj

By being one of the first project engineering companies to have established its own R&D centre, Praj demonstrated its commitment to continuous improvement of process efficiencies and to the quality of the equipment it has installed. Within the company, the distribution of work between engineering, manufacturing and projects is equitable. However, to the company, the importance of manufacturing is less than that in other companies. Hence, the question of a learning curve-type cost reduction in manufacturing is of no great significance in Praj.

Insistence on High Quality

One of the striking things about the successful companies studied is their insistence on offering products of the highest quality. To ensure that this happens, these companies had taken elaborate care right from the beginning.

- Even as a small formulation unit, not only did Sun undertake simpler tests in its QC laboratory, but also acquired expensive machines such as the HPLC. One seldom sees such equipment with SSI formulators. And this in Vapi's ethos, a town thickly populated with SSI formulators. Cut-throat competition among formulators is and has been the order of the day here. As one Sun officer put it, the single most important factor contributing to Sun's growth was its unwavering commitment to high quality.
- Dr Reddy's Laboratories has enjoyed a steady reputation for technical excellence and won several awards on this score. The USP of its formulations has been its quality.
- Orchid established itself as a supplier of bulk drugs of such high quality that not only did it replace other Indian producers of cephalosporins within and outside the country as the preferred supplier, but also became a benchmark of quality.
- Sumangal innovated on continuous modification of the product features, imparting it the hallmark of cultural quality which now makes for its complete ethnic identity.
- Mastek was willing to and did offer performance as well as time-of-completion guarantees of its custom-made software development projects, to the extent that it was willing to take penalty on these score, and that in the economic ethos of the early 1980s.
- V-Guard offered a superior product and even as a wholly unheard-of-make, had the guts to price its products above the established brands, thus emphasising its quality.

Several dimensions of quality are involved here—product features and attributes, durability, adherence to established standards, punctuality, etc. What becomes critical for a given company depends upon its product and business. The point is to win a reputation for high quality and reliability and to exploit that as the single most effective weapon in competing.

Other Such Examples

There are several examples of growth occurring because of the focal unit's unwavering attention to the logistics of manufacturing, purchase, etc. And its commitment to quality. I mention just two instances from the post-1990s entrepreneurs.

- Core, the IV fluid maker who achieved runaway success from 1989 to 1995, did so by remarkable commitment to manufacturing and distribution logistics. The attention to purchase logistics was so thorough that it could contain the plastic cost to the original levels over this period despite a war, rupee devaluation and inflation thereafter. The attention to manufacturing spoke of high dedication and achieved kudos for the company not only from buyers but also from the very vendors of the machines. Finally, the company managed its overall logistics so well that it reduced the (imputed) working capital costs per unit of manufactured products by almost 50 per cent, as the volumes multiplied over a hundred-fold during the same time!
- A small company in the competitive business of making light filaments, VWF insisted upon its quality standards and evolved an elaborate system of tracing responsibility of a given lot to identifiable individuals. This system of improvement in quality led to dramatic results and the company could profitably exploit export markets for these products, as the domestic competition became too hot due to undercutting and long credit periods.

The foregoing discussion is summarised in Table 6.1.

TABLE 6.1
Logistics in Successful Companies

Sl. No.	Name	Choice of Tech	Size	Pace	Efforts	Importance
1	Sun	2	2	1	Q.2	2
2	DRL	3	1	2	2	2
3	Orchid	1	1	1	1	1
4	Biocon	2, 3	2	2	Q.2	2
5	Mastek	1	2	2	–	–
6	Sudha	2	2	2	1	1
7	V-Guard	3	2	2	–	–
8	Praj	1, 3	2	2	1	2
9	Sumangal	2	2	3	2	2
10	Ashima	1	1	1	1	1

- Choice of technology: state of the art 1, usual 2, own devep. 3
- Size of plant: large compared to sales 1, small 2
- Pace of expansion: fast 1, slow 2, matched with sales 3
- Efforts for upgrading quality and or efficiencies: efforts focused on quality not so much as efficiency Q.2, efforts emphasised 1, silent 2
- Importance to manufacturing department within the company-high 1, normal 2

7

Organisational Issues and Management Styles

It is All in the Mind

At a couple of places earlier in this text I have referred to the 'typical mindset of the small-industry owner'. I wish to devote some discussion to this question before coming to the issues of organisational culture and managerial style. I am aware of the dangers of creating stereotypes, and the fact that often while attempting to characterise an ideal type, one merely caricatures a stereotype. Let me then portray the work ethos of the small-industry owner and thereafter, almost in a justifying tone, enumerate the attributes of the mindset of SSI owners.

SSI owners come from two dominant backgrounds: trade or engineering. The entrepreneur in the first class inherit strong elements of mercantile capitalism from his or her background. The entrepreneur of the second type has strong preoccupations with a technical subject. There is also a third category of a professional 'management' type, a la Handas of Core, Ashank and colleagues at Mastek, K.R. Rao of Orchid,

Pankaj Sethi of Nimbus Communications, Rajiv Agarwal of Nexus Equity, etc. This last group appears to be of a more recent vintage and I do not know if the sample is large enough already to characterise its ideal type.

Trader-turned-industrialist

First the justification for the mindset. A trader trades in someone else's goods and his inherent commitment to it is small. The quality assurance as well as servicing is someone else's headache. He can quickly change the goods he actually trades: the clothier till yesterday can become a hardware merchant in a fortnight. His main investment is in working capital. Credit periods given and enjoyed as well as the width and depth of his inventory influence that. His margins are limited to a small percentage plus such trade discounts as the manufacturer offers. He must manage all the costs of being in the business and make a decent living. He thus focuses on controlling and reducing his immediate cash costs. The manpower needed is just that of hey-yous, the *'seth ka aadmis'*. He has neither an occasion nor any grounds for delegation. In fact, delegation is deemed to be fraught with dangers. Delegation, if any, is done only for family members involved in the business. Often, delegation is adopted in a convenient manner either for putting off or avoiding a commitment. (It sounds hilarious, but I know several brothers—call them pairs of Ram and Laxman—together running a business. Whenever some unfortunate salesman comes for collection and asks for Ram bhaiya, the person at the counter says that Ram bhaiya is away and since he deals with all bills, it cannot be settled in his absence. And this happens if the salesman is new and even if the person at the counter is Ram bhaiya! Traders consider this smart behaviour.)

And the trader-turned-industrialist has spent half a lifetime in this ethos, or seen his elders doing this. That is why the mindset, possibly fully justified in the prevailing business environment of a small industrialist, appears completely normal to him.

The SSI owner coming from a trade background is likely, in fact more than likely, to try and thrive on 'me-too' products. If in his judgement the demand–supply mismatch exists in established products, he will surely enter that line. He seldom worries about issues of core competence. He is perfectly at ease in simultaneously running, and for decades, factories manufacturing very different lines, the lines having no connection to each other in terms of processes, customers, raw materials or employee skills. A successful SSI owner running a factory connected with metal powders, if in this mindset, could be perfectly comfortable investing his surplus cash and time in marble cutting and polishing, finding nothing inappropriate in it. And this could go on for decades, the third line quite conceivably being a frozen fruit factory!

He is prone to be myopic about product quality, customer relations and servicing. He is preoccupied with managing the laws rather than obeying them. He is often willing to play with reality a little to suit the regulatory laws such as labour laws or fiscal laws. He is most apt to compete on price and longer credit periods rather than product features and quality of service.

Technocrat-turned-industrialist

The focus here is on the first-generation technocrat who has no family background of trade. This guy is likely to be very bright and he thoroughly understands his field. It is likely to be a narrow field such as metal coating of surfaces or underwater welding. He knows almost everything about it. The chances are that he is also very well informed about a whole range of other subjects, in the manner of someone who wins quiz contests where one is asked how many hair a monkey has in its nose. Such precise, accurate irrelevant and trivial information helps you to prove yourself one up over your peers, to top exams and show your fellow engineers they are wrong. (Scott Adam's engineer in Dilbert is a good portrait of this type.) He is apt to assess everyone else by the amount of technical knowledge they have. This can often not be much, at least compared to a specialist. Hence to him they are obviously thick, dumb, stupid and no good.

The technocrat works in a reputed firm for a length of time and becomes established as a 'practical engineer'. As a successful technocrat, he is apt to be impatient, direct, naive and at times simple. If one can stand his penchant for accurate but irrelevant information, his narrow perspective and technocratic superiority, he is good company and quite sweet. Sweet at times even as a boss!

He then decides to go on his own. He creates the best possible technical infrastructure his money can buy, possibly exhausting all his resources or at least stretching them significantly. He might therefore start with a working capital handicap. This chap is not broken in the business world. He dislikes the management of money, dealing with customers on non-technical matters, getting your payments passed, managing the myriad government functionaries. His manipulative partners have an easy time with him. He does not understand or at any rate has no use for all this fuss about team building, delegation, communication, interpersonal relations and so on. He thinks this HRD stuff to be mushy nonsense. He is often in for a traumatic shock owing either to acute funds crisis or non-cooperation of employees.

(The advantage is, since he is very bright and solid, once he decides that running a successful business is like solving a quiz, he will get down to it adopting the most fancy techniques ever heard. He will listen actively all the time, collaborate with everyone and their grandmothers, build teams with a vengeance, and furiously motivate people 36 hours a day. While also worrying about the last paisa in managing working capital.)

There is absolutely nothing wrong in any one facet of either of the mindsets taken in isolation. In its totality it becomes a problem. Floating a dummy unit merely to save on some taxes may be a smart move in the short run, but doing it time and again and then wasting time managing the complex accounts of 20 firms on paper would mean that one would never have the time to focus on issues of growth of the empire one wishes to see. Not delegating to an engineer matters that concern him may not cause much harm in the short run, but not allowing anyone to do anything at all without a clear green signal from the entrepreneur would paralyse the enterprise at its critical growth phase. The problems come when the company has the opportunity or the potential to grow but the mindset comes in the way. The increasing complexity of business demands decentralisation of decision making, or at least substantial increase in the participation of key functionaries, but the entrepreneur may not be willing at all to delegate or even to listen to others. Technical expertise in the form of non-dispersed specific technical knowledge may come only if the persons bringing it are given due recognition and say in running the company, and again the entrepreneur may fight shy of involving them. Growth might mean substantially augmented financial muscle, which could come only by persuading alert investors and bankers to invest. This could happen only if a gray zone behaviour is given up and transparency is increased in the company, but this could be culturally incompatible with the entrepreneur. Simultaneous engagement in several assignments may mean much greater formalisation in functions such as quoting for a new project, hiring new staff, etc. And formalisation may lead to reduced control of the boss if he were earlier the 'star' model of the organisation.

In most of the companies studied, this mindset question came up. More often than not, it was brought up by the key entrepreneur himself. At times by others. Different people brought out different facets and not much is to be gained in specific attribution of views to individuals. What emerges in a general summary form is somewhat on the following lines.

The 'SSI mindset' is restrictive in that it puts too much pressure on one individual. It is self-defeating in that it distracts and dilutes the managerial focus that is needed to tackle issues that concern a growing enterprise. It is counter-productive in that it discourages expansion of the total capability of the firm because of the inhibition of the desirable new entrants to join the firm at all. What is needed for transition to medium/large firm and further to grow on its steam into a potential industrial giant is the emphasis

- on organisational routines rather than individual predilections
- on teamwork rather than individual hard work
- on trust and collaboration
- on openness and transparency, on formalisation and structures for decision making and on a commonly shared vision among all the people

As the MD of one of the companies studied said, 'By God's grace I have made some money. I do not want to run this company merely because I want to make more money. I have a dream and only those who understand and share my dream will be wholeheartedly committed to work with me. I have then to sell my dream to them!' Most entrepreneurs associated with these companies mentioned how their decision making styles and mindset changed either during or just before the period of transition of their business to a medium/large organisation. The external manifestations (which could of course be mere empty forms without substance if adopted merely for public consumption!) of this phenomenon are what we will now discuss.

Form of the Organisation

A majority of these firms are in the widely held company form of organisation, though the original pioneer could still, and usually does retain a substantial stake. Firms that did not start in this mode converted to it within a decade of starting.

- Sun is a listed and actively quoted public limited company since 1994, though the pioneer holds a very large stake in it (10).
- DRL was a public limited company right from the start and is now widely held.
- Orchid is a widely held company since start.
- Praj is a widely held company since 1993 (7).
- Ashima is a widely held company since 1992.
- Mastek is a widely held company (10).

The figures in brackets indicate the number of years within which the firm converted itself to a WHC. Sudha, Biocon and V-Guard are public limited companies, though not traded actively on any exchange. They have not made a public issue. They are closely held. Sumangal is a private limited company.

In the post-1992 sharemarket bubble, a whole range of companies went public and made IPOs. So one might be tempted to ask what is new about these companies becoming public. What is new is that virtually no company went public (in legal form) primarily to garner money from the market. They might have made public issues for different reasons, but they did have the wherewithal to undertake investments using other sources of finance at those times. Sun went public primarily because the management thought that this was one sure way of ensuring that the 'SSI mindset' would be given up in favour of growth-oriented organisational culture. The same is true of other companies. The proportion of money that was obtained from the public has formed a small part of the capital employed by these companies. The logic, it seems, is that the management:

- desires to run a large business, to become 'big', to 'fulfil a dream'
- comes to the conclusion that the organisational culture needs to change from a small-enterprise mindset to a formal, professional growth-oriented one

- finds that the legal requirement of being a public limited company automatically facilitates this cultural change
- converts the company into a public limited one
- feels that if it can use the money from an IPO in well-identified projects, it should make an IPO

The interesting thing is that the track record of the remaining four companies (Sumangal, Sudha, Biocon and V-Guard) is such that they would make a successful maiden public issue, and yet they decide not to make one. Thus what is common to all the companies is that virtually none of them suffered from the cheap greed of hundreds of other fly-by-night operators who made an issue, gobbled up money from a gullible public, very probably diverted it and then forgot about doing a decent business! This common trait itself is remarkable and possibly unusual in the current Indian business ethos.

Systems of Work and Extent of Formalisation

An important aspect of an organisation is the way things are done in it. The extent of formalisation in information flow, decision making, allocation and use of resources and coordination is indicative of how far the firm has moved from the SSI-mindset. Firms that remain highly informally managed, with minimum formal reporting, high dependence on and hence control of one individual, are very likely still in the SSI mindset. Let us call this the Stage 1 of organisational development of a firm.

It is likely that what happens as growth occurs is that a formal structure begins to emerge with its attendant formal information and decision systems. At first this remains fairly informal, much information being shared verbally with little efforts to develop an organisational memory. Decisions, though in principle now delegated, are taken informally with justifications that are not formally articulated. As one Mastek executive said, initially their quotation would be based on two or three factors: a broad understanding of the job involved, the need to get more work and the feeling that long-term customer relations are important. The decision would be expressed as *chalo* inventory management system *ka ek lakh mang lete hain*—let us ask for a lakh for the inventory management system'. There was no specific attempt to estimate the programmer-days required, cost per programmer per day being applied to it, etc. Similar things happened elsewhere. In other companies too, the initial days of emergence of structure are characterised by relatively informal decision making. This is the second phase. Sumangal and Sudha appear to be in this phase; interestingly they are among the older companies studied. Gradually, the need

- for appearing to be taking similar if not uniform stand across different customer, suppliers, employees, etc.
- to make decision making both more predictable and efficient
- for an organisation memory

all together cause formalisation in information and decision flows in terms of documentation, forms, standard operating procedures, manuals and the like. The newly fashionable desire for ISO certification becomes a very positive influence on formalisation. Slowly the role contents become less dependent on persons occupying them. Things become more system driven. The size of the organisation may not allow full blooded bureaucracy to set in, but there are a lot of forms and reports all over. This then is the third phase. DRL and Biocon are in this phase. The entrepreneur continues to be quite central to decision making but efforts to reduce his role are actively under way. Thus in DRL, as the MD said, 'So far we depended too much on Dr Reddy to tell us what we should do and we grew because he knows this business and so could identify the new product we should get into, could help us with the technology, etc. Now we need to start doing these things ourselves, with the active involvement of everyone.'

The organisation continues to grow, geographically, in width of the product line, number of facilities and employment. Perhaps new specialisations become essential. The fourth phase is the one where documentation and formalisation become a strong need since their absence threaten the smooth functioning of the organisation. There now are formal department heads, who are encouraged to take initiative so far as their functions are concerned; routine coordination needs are met through cross-functional teams on which the entrepreneur may not sit at all; for a department the word of the department head starts mattering as much if not more than that of the MD; the MD himself/herself seldom wishes to go over their head; etc. This organisation is completely formalised now (and could conceivably degenerate into a bureaucracy). Sun, Praj and Mastek have reached this phase, with the touch of a little sadness about the extent of formalisation being expressed by a few of the old-timers.

The final phase observed in my sample is characterised by high decentralisation, highly formal reporting and communication between such decentralised units, extensive and intensive use of IT and near-complete depersonification of management. The MD starts appearing as an occupant of just one role rather than the all-powerful demi-god. Decisions are taken in a professional manner, using the appropriate techno-managerial techniques for information, data collation and analysis. The firm behaves like a large one. Orchid and Ashima have reached this stage, Orchid much earlier than one would have thought, perhaps because of the background of the key entrepreneur in costing, MIS, etc.

Managerial Styles and Blunders

The question with which the investigation of this research problem began was whether the successful companies manage themselves in a manner distinct from thousands of other SSI units set up around the same time by other entrepreneurs, but which have either fallen by the wayside or have been overtaken by events. And to what extent did pure chance play a part in this success of the companies. I have repeatedly contended that a majority of the small industrial units which stagnate or even become sick do so because they commit many of the 'blunders' discussed in *How not to ruin your small industry*. The starting point was to put forth two possibilities. Either the successful companies did not ever commit any of these blunders, or having committed these, they quickly learnt and found ways of getting over the ill-effects of the blunders. So it is instructive to see whether the companies committed any of the eight blunders discussed in the first chapter. Let me start with Sun.

To start with, Sun was dependent on only the east Indian market for psychotropic drugs, which is how the company began. The company shifted to Vapi because the management thought that this established pharma belt was a better place for a pharma company. The company systematically reduced its dependence in the east Indian market. It then reduced its dependence on one therapy. Thus over a time, it achieved a degree of product and market diversification. No traces of Blunder 1 here.

The company had been adding fixed assets quickly, but incrementally and never so dramatically as to cause a massive liquidity crunch. No Blunder 2 either. Sun certainly did not speculate on raw material prices and the like. I do not think I have any evidence of Sun doing informal, cash business. So no Blunder 3 or 4. Yes, they floated more than one firm. The Halol company (Unimed) was set up as a separate firm, there is a distribution company and there is an export company. The logic being that the Halol firm was owned by relatives and friends in which Shanghvi himself had little stake, that it was used as a production base and that the dealings were at an arm's length and on the same terms as with other third-party suppliers. The possibility of them joining him in expanding Sun existed at the time of the company's inception, there was the potential loss of Sun's SSI status which was a consideration in 1985. But no efforts were spared to build up Sun's brands, market strength and corporate image. And everything was managed in an above-the-board manner. Sun did not commit any of the other blunders.

DRL too floated too many firms. In fact when Standard Organic Limited became successful, both Anji Reddy and Chandrasekhar Reddy floated many firms between 1984 and 1985, the two having made up their minds to separate. Anji Reddy wished to pursue things of technical excellence while his partner was more interested in commercial success. Amongst the firms floated were Cheminor which made its mark in making the bulk drug Ibuprofen, DRL itself, a leasing and finance company which collected deposits from the public, even a computer peripheral unit. As recent as in 1993, they started a 100 per cent EOU making halogen lamps! But all these unrelated activities were started for the short-term consideration of taking advantage of the tax laws and with not too much loss of focus from the main business. The promoters are quite candid that the peripheral, unrelated businesses have been or would be sold, and that the related companies would be merged soon.

Orchid has tended to invest too quickly and substantially in fixed assets such as hardware for the factory business, but it does not fear a liquidity crisis since its working capital need is not too high. However, whether exclusive dependence on cephalosporins becomes dysfunctional is a moot point. The company is certain that there is a large enough market which will last and hence its focus on one class of drugs. But there is hardly any asset specificity. With certain relatively minor hardware changes, the company can shift to manufacture of any other bulk drug. No other blunder is to be imputed and the company offers a good example of brilliant techno-managerial professionalism.

Mastek has more current than fixed assets and has still to worry about liquidity owing to its strategy of starting local subsidiaries in host countries. These companies have assets that are not large enough to give them the ability to raise local debts and hence must depend on the parent company for their working capital. Its emphasis to remain lean and mean in India therefore makes sense. Mastek might have tended to depend excessively on the Ingress-based business in the domestic market and on the east Asian business for the group as a whole, but the problems of excessive dependence are not insurmountable. There are six firms in the group, five of which are in five different countries and that has been a well thought-out strategy. The recruitment focus has shifted to the second-rung institutions as youngsters from the IITs and IIMs have their eyes riveted irrevocably on the west, thus causing substantial employee turnover. They do have rigorous employees' quality assurance at the entry level and within the second-rung source, competence is the only criterion to pick up a new recruit.

Biocon too has five firms now: the parent company, another one owned equally by Biocon and Unilevers, a contract research company, a 100 per cent EOU and more recently a new business—a company that will engage in large-scale manufacture of drugs. This seems to be justified on account of the peculiar nature of the business or ownership of each one of them. None is a dummy firm created solely to avoid some tax or labour law. The company does not appear close to any other blunder.

Sudha, though close to the SSI mindset, is managed without committing any blunder, except perhaps in the choice of employees. The employees appear to be from the local community, possibly having kinship with the key entrepreneur. But in fairness it must be stated that in a rural location in the middle of nowhere, the choice for the bulk of the staff must restrict itself to the local community. In recent years, the company seems to have invested substantially in fixed assets, leading for the first time to book losses in the last financial year. Since high depreciation and finance charges are bound to be high in the first complete year after investments are made, this does not seem to be an unexpected or even a difficult problem to solve. Other than these two areas, there is little reason to think that Sudha is close to any blunder. What is surprising is its scrupulous avoidance of speculation and of floating many firms, so common to enterprises in commodity lines in far-flung areas.

Sumangal's case is special in that it started cautiously, investing slowly in fixed assets. It used others' presses for years for printing calendars, its only product. The case throws insufficient light on the style of management, type of employees and financial administration, but I am more intrigued by its choice of new activities (Internet-based service and participating in events such as Advantage Maharashtra). I do not think its management suggests proximity to any blunder.

Praj tended to depend on one line for a length of time but diversified into non-molasses-based distilleries quite early on to avoid excessive dependence on this one line. Subsequent diversification appears to have been designed to reduce this dependence even further. The company certainly has not over-invested in fixed assets or indulged in hiring employees for any reason other than their competence. Praj possibly has an enviable strength in process engineering design and commissioning, arising out of its formidable employee skills.

V-Guard used to operate fairly informally without keeping too much record and without even hiring an accountant. It was under the impression, subsequently ratified by the apex court, that the responsibility for payment of excise duty was with the manufacturer, and since much of its production was obtained by genuine sub-contractors (who were not just dummy firms, but de jure as well as de facto different enterprises), it had to worry about its tax liability. A massive and expensive litigation jerked the company out of this informal business practice and it hired the best professionals to design its elaborate accounting system thereafter. Aside from this blunder, V-Guard does not seem to have committed any other.

Finally, Ashima started in the classic SSI mindset, setting up more firms than it could count on its hands, but these were not paper firms. These were business ventures engaged in assorted, unrelated businesses—from melmoware to polyester texturising. Another potential blunder was the exclusive dependence on the suppliers of polyester filament yarn. However, once Ashima decided to come out in the sun, it shrugged off the past and went whole hog in consolidation of facilities, development of technical competence and building the corporate image. Ashima too could be thought as having invested very substantially, but working capital is not a major source of worry.

Thus the most common act among the ten successful companies is floating too many firms. Since these are exceptionally well-managed companies, the boot could be on the other foot and I might be mistaken in calling this a blunder. Before I retract from my original position, I should like to point out that to me what is a blunder is the following very specific set of decisions:

> A firm starts floating many firms merely to escape excise, sales tax, labour, pollution or one such law in force; the new firm is a dummy firm—every thing about it except its registration number, sales tax number and perhaps electric connection is fictitious; the same set of employees work for both or all the firms; the accounts of both the firms are managed 'creatively' to minimise cumulative tax liability of the entrepreneur and also to access cheap institutional finance when none of the firmlets have sufficiently long and solid financial track record.

It is evident that none of these successful firms committed this blunder.

TABLE 7.1
Organisational Issues and Management Style in Successful Companies

Name	Org. Form	Control & Delegation	People Met	Systems & Formalisation	Overall Judgement	Blunders Committed
Sun	WHC,**,2	2 followed by 3	1	2	2	Many firms
DRL	WHC*,1	1, 3 tried	2	3	1	Many firms
Orchid	WHC*,1	2	1	1	2	–
Biocon	CHC	1	1	3	2	Many firms
Sudha	CHC	1	3	5	3	Over-investment
Mastek	WHC*,2	2 followed by 3	1	2	2	Excessive dependence
Praj	WHC*,1	2 followed by 3	1	2	2	Excessive dependence
Sumangal	CHC	1	2	4	1	Borrowings?
V-Guard	CHC	1	2	3	1	Informal business
Ashima	WHC*,2	1 followed by 3	1	1	2	Many firms

Notes

Org Form: WHC means widely held company, the number of stars indicates the extent of stake held by key promoter and the number following that indicates the number of years after starting business the firm became WHC; 1 meaning less than 5 years and 2 meaning above 5. CHC means closely held company, whether private, deemed public or public

Control: 1 control (final and frequently sought say) by family or entrepreneur, 2 by the team of entrepreneurs and 3 being formalised in a structured manner, delegated to professionals

People hired (and met with): 1: professionals oriented towards organisation; 2: professionals transiting from personal loyalty to organisation orientation; 3: strongly kinship/family based, under social patronage of entrepreneurs

Systems of work and extent of formalisation: 1: highly formal, structured, documented, IT based, with formal MIS, etc. 2: formal and structured, IT being introduced, documentation may be incomplete 3: transiting from undocumented to relatively more formal 4: emerging from entrepreneur dependent to stable routines, but undocumented 5: undocumented, entrepreneur dependent and possibly quite informal and ad hoc

Overall Judgement: 1: highly entrepreneur centred, lion cub style, aggressive 2: team based or at least more participative than 1, purposive and task oriented, systematic; close to fox mode 3: entrepreneur dominated, cautious and lizard model

8

Management of Human Resources in the Successful Companies

Let me begin with a qualifying comment. It is not my place to comment on whether the companies in the chosen sample had created a nurturing environment through sound HR management. I wonder whether I have enough data to comment on it either. What I will do is to describe the management practices in these companies to the extent my database permits and draw patterns, if any, from these descriptions. Seven processes—namely recruitment, induction, training and development, performance appraisal, career path progression and management of group processes—make for the complete HR management. These are generic processes, necessary in all organisations. Obviously all of them engage in these. The way they handle these processes determines the quality of their HR management. Then there are symbolic actions and rituals: annual get togethers, house journals, picnics and sports. Since these were observed in almost every company, we will not discuss these.

Sun recruited persons initially through word of mouth but started adopting formal procedures almost within a couple of years of establishment. One employee recalls how he was caught young, just finishing college, given a friendly but incisive gruelling for finding out his inner abilities and then hired. From 1989 onwards (after about seven years of existence), most of the personnel functions started getting systematised. The company's recruitment ad now carries the line 'Join the winning team!'—stressing both winning as well as team spirit. While choosing a person the emphasis is on ensuring that he is compatible with the rest of the team, able to work hard and under pressure, and subscribes to trust and openness.

Sun has a remarkable system of looking after its employees. An old employee once resigned after putting in a few years' service, believing that he had developed an allergy to some materials being used in the factory. He recalls how the 'MD himself took me to the best dermatologist, the sort I could not afford' and had him examined. When it transpired that his skin problem was not of allergic origin, he was told that he could leave if he so desired, but not for that reason. An equally remarkable incident was that of a new recruit who developed acute renal problem. From the wording of the application for leave, the superior judged the nature of the problem, shifted the boy from the nursing home where he was sinking and arranged for a kidney transplant. 'I literally owe my life to the company', said the young man to me.

As a large company, Sun has to now sort out the issues caused by distance: physical, organisational and social—among staff and between staff and management. It has had one labour dispute that entailed work stoppage but was resolved amicably without involving courts or labour commissioners. Sun has regular training programmes in functional areas, conducted by experts within the company. Consultants help them with some programmes. A weekly seminar series offers scope for employees to come and present what they have done and this is viewed as a welcome opportunity to share achievements, ideas and experiences. Sun's employee turnover is modest, the highest turnover being in the field of sales personnel, who are lured by multinational companies with exorbitant pay packages. But many of those who go thus are said to return.

Dr Reddy's Laboratories has a large workforce now. Given Anji Reddy's background, it is easy to understand that technical professionals find DRL an attractive employer. The company in general and the research foundation in particular are taken to be excellent places to learn and to develop careers. Anji Reddy has always been an exponent of freedom and of liberal financial support to researchers and has followed this policy in his own company. The company has been a grooming ground for many successful pharma executives. The technical staff join the firm, learn the trade and then become attractive recruits for smaller companies which at a point in time mushroomed around Hyderabad. Several also leave—with Anji Reddy's blessings—to pursue advanced courses abroad. The turnover is around 15 per cent even in the salesforce. It is the new recruits in sales who are most prone to quit; after a few years in the company people generally do not leave.

Dr Anji Reddy is firmly committed to the philosophy of human resources development. He has donated liberally to the Academy of Human Resources established in Hyderabad. DRL has focused on creating a caring work culture. It has taken up the huge task of involvement and mobilisation of the entire workforce in making the company a global pharmaceutical player. The Managing Director himself addresses the workforce and staff to explain the company mission and to involve them in the continuous process of improvement. HRD efforts are also said to be focused on improving communication among staff and between staff and management. The problem of distance is not very serious here. The workers' trade union is quite strong, though because of its ability to pay above average wages there has been no cause for collective action here. Internal training effort is focused on technical matters while external sources are used for managerial training.

There is no gainsaying the fact that Anji Reddy has emerged as a paternalistic leader of the organisation. For many years, he was the sole repertoire of decision-making savvy in all crucial matters: choice of products, technologies, markets, leaving implementation to those who had been with him for years, were competent and knew precisely what he wanted. The second generation is slowly taking command even though there was some reluctance in taking initiative in contributing to decision making. The MD Sathish Reddy feels that they had depended too long on the sagacity of Anji Reddy, that they had to learn to put their heads together and take decisions, and that this will make the company maintain and reach even greater heights.

Orchid is a very young organisation. Its very conception and launch have occurred in a team mode. While Rao has taken greater financial stake, others have given their best to the company. Given the team approach to decision making, there is much emphasis on transparency and openness. Rao and his senior management colleagues have ensured that youngsters take responsibility while also developing their own careers. Orchid financially supports any initiative taken by the staff for own career development. The recruitment process is fully formalised and people are chosen without any extraneous considerations. The fact that no two members of the board are related to each other, that the entrepreneurial team has come together not for familial but purely professional links and that there is much focus on openness and formalisation has ensured that the company hires people only for their abilities. The HRD function has started relatively recently, as is to be expected in a new company. The concern is to manage the expectations as well as the likely disappointments of youngsters, who will grow together professionally and look for career advancement around the same time.

Mastek too began in a team mode. When they got together at IIMA, Sundar was about 25, Vasan a year younger and Ketan practically in his teens. Ashank, 27, was the oldest. The team has always regarded Ashank as being the first among equals. They never had destabilising ego clashes. Later when Sudhakar joined, replacing Vasan who went abroad, the same arrangement continued. Later, Ashank became the natural choice for the position of the head of Mastek. To quote Ketan, 'Ashank has a flair for dealing with outsiders and that helped.'

The four members of the pioneering team were young, professionally trained, committed to making a success of their venture. With sound academic background from prestigious institutions, they were natural role models for other computer professionals beginning their careers. Sundar took the initial initiative to attract bright engineers seeking computer careers. Ashank took charge of recruitment, keeping personal control on selection tests, scores, etc. He also took great interest in the new recruits, spending time with them at professional as well as social planes. Several individuals interviewed spoke of their close interaction with the team and with Ashank. Frugality—forced by erratic flow of work and of payment—became a sort of game, as there were no demonstrative signs of status. When all the engineers came together and there was a shortage of chairs, someone stood, and it could be, would be, one of the pioneer team. This combination of a warm human touch, informality and professional competence became the ground on which the employee-related policy evolved.

Later, the company had to compete in hiring computer professionals. The first indication was the western affliction affecting the youngsters from IIMs and IITs. A 23-year-old does get starry-eyed at the prospect of migrating to the never-never land. The company executives explained that the shorter the time in which a software engineer would be sent abroad by an employer, the better chances the employer had of getting people. Mastek itself never believed in the bodyshopping trade of the software line and started losing out in the race for recruitment. It then shifted focus to the second-rung institutions such as the regional engineering colleges. The stability of the young programming staff is still a major issue Mastek has been grappling with. Its reorganisation in 'software factory' form raised some issues of imbalance in demand and supply of programming staff across these factories. Worse, no one seems to want to work on Indian clients! The other issues are those thrown up by growth. Formalisation has meant procedures, paperwork and meetings. The older lot who are used to informal, trust-based working environment find this galling. Finally, as the computing and software technology has changed rapidly there is the question of insecurity born out of a feeling of redundance among those who were in the thick of things some years back. These issues are being addressed without coercion, but with participation, consensus and mutuality. The basic tenets of professionalism and a warm human touch remain. What is most striking is the willingness to talk about these matters openly and across the various levels of the organisation.

Biocon presents the image of a professionally managed organisation. There are several women heading various departments. Staff are exceptionally well qualified. The environment is informal, everyone calling everyone else by the first names, etc. The work seems to be done in a very structured and purposive manner, with minimal informal pleasantries. Everything you see is shining and gleaming. The front office decor is expensive but tasteful. (The decor, etc., have a minor relationship with the HRD policy, but I seek to create an image of the company.) Definitely the 'modern organisation'. Staff is hired through formal mechanisms. Salaries are well above average and compare well with the alternatives available to the staff. Biocon has even adopted the ESOP mode of compensation. Employee turnover is low. Among the small set of organisations seriously engaged in bio-technology research in India, only a few offer work environment better than Biocon, said one executive. And this small universe is now well known to the staff, so the turnover is not on account of people migrating to other companies but their going abroad for higher studies, etc. With the start of Helix, the latest company in the Biocon family, spaces for growth have already been created for the young staff.

Praj began excelling in another technical field of process engineering, a field which is strictly the domain of engineers. And in this line it engaged in significant technology development. Three-fourths of its 400 employees are chemical or mechanical engineers. The management cadre constitutes of 60 employees. The corporate management team, comprising the CMD, Deputy MD and 15 top managers, governs the strategic decisions such as the choice of product lines, technologies and resource allocation. Teams of professionals at varying levels assist in the formulation of the corporate goals and policies on the one hand and translate them into action on the other. Teamwork is again the key in Praj. There are many 'old-timers' in this 14-year-old company. Since the company grew rapidly, the team size was small till recently and there was much emphasis on informality. Now with its growing size, adoption of systematic and stylised work has become necessary and a central issue perceived by the company HRD manager pertains to striking the right balance between systematic management and informality.

The second, and this is my own prognostication not articulated by any company executive, is to manage the middle-aging of a large number of technically oriented competent professionals who joined and reached positions of authority before crossing their thirties. Praj never sold itself as a high-paying organisation, but as one where responsibility and professional growth were the main rewards. As the company matures, the pace of growth may relatively reduce and the question of middle-aging will come up.

Praj hires its engineers through the Graduate Engineering Trainees (GET) programme. It has stayed away from the campuses of management institutions for quite some time. The company arranges technical training for its engineers in Indian as well as foreign institutions. It has tied up with the Tata Management Training Centre for management training, particularly for those who are assuming general management roles.

Ashima too believes in complete professionalism and informality. Chintan Parikh belongs to a business family. Yet he has consciously avoided inviting any of his family members on the board. Ashima places a great deal of emphasis on hiring people with relevant experience, particularly if hired at middle levels. Being a whiz-kid in finance or computers does not automatically qualify a person to be hired unless he or she has demonstrated evidence of having applied the knowledge to the textile sector. There is a focus on constant learning and renewal. Technical as well as behavioural training is in-house. The HRD process is concentrated towards making Ashima an organisation that is driven by logic and a desire for learning. Openness, professionalism and logic are three central values.

The cases of Sudha, V-Guard and Sumangal do not provide the material required to comment on HRD practices there.

Inference

The foregoing clearly indicates that the successful companies share the values of informal work culture, thorough professionalism, open and transparent work systems and focus on constant development of individuals' potential. Five (Sun, DRL, Mastek, Praj and Ashima) of the seven companies on whom we have sufficient information have positioned senior personnel in charge of HRD. In at least three (Mastek, DRL and Praj), the key entrepreneur himself takes a keen interest in HRD. Most have shifted to formal procedures for recruitment. Virtually all of them have lower employee turnover than their peers in the industry. Some companies such as Sun pride themselves on the humane and concerned approach towards colleagues while demanding high degree of performance and hard work. Except when the key entrepreneur is regarded as a father figure, as in the case of DRL, executives in most companies are at pains to emphasise that exchange of information and decision-related views within are delinked from hierarchy and this democratic approach to pre-decision discussion includes even the CEO.

There is fair convergence of views of enlightened opinion today that management of human resources is a critical function in organisations. It is implied if not explicitly stated that given the same set of employees and managers, 'good' HR management can make for a vibrant, dynamic and outward-looking organisation while 'insensitive' HR management can cause it to become a stagnant and oppressive jail the inmates of which seek to be elsewhere all the time. While the profitability and growth of organisations obviously depend on a whole lot of other factors, good HR management has the salutary effect of making it a sustainable social entity. That by itself makes for conducive work environment in which people are encouraged to perform.

There perhaps is no fixed recipe for good HR management, but the end result is amenable to description. An organisation that practises good HR management is characterised by greater openness, sharing, trust and collaboration. Teamwork is the accepted behaviour pattern here. Individuals working in this organisation feel a sense of belonging to it. The talents of individuals are recognised early. There is a proactive approach to providing opportunities to individuals to reach their full potential. In consequence, the turnover among employees is low and average organisational longevity is high. (It is possible to argue that a general paucity of employment opportunities cause these effects on turnover and longevity. While true about low and medium skill levels, for many lines, especially the professional lines, there is no paucity of employment opportunity.) When judged on these criteria, human resources in these successful companies seem to be managed in an enlightened manner.

9

So What is New in the Management of the Successful Companies?

The business of management of a small industry poses a paradox. Since it is commonly, if not invariably, a single-product, single-facility kind of a business the complexity is low. And yet this seemingly low complexity proves difficult to handle for small entrepreneurs, as they must do so in the absence or at least paucity of material, financial and managerial resources. Starting from such a situation, the companies studied here have done well. They have graduated to becoming medium companies with respectable turnover, some with formidable market reputation and presence. What exactly did they do?

By looking at the way these companies managed marketing, finance and organisational issues, I tried to see the nitty gritty of their basic management styles. It appears that most took up products that were either new or at their growth stage in the PLC. I found that most were conservative in the way they managed their finances. Most employed highly professional (frankly, large company-type) manpower. Now let us focus on the new things they did, whether in marketing, production processes or any other field. This will offer important lessons to other SMEs. By the word 'new', I mean acts that were innovative or at least not commonly seen in the management of similarly situated companies. There undoubtedly is a judgement involved here. It is possible that I might attribute novelty or originality to actions that are in fact quite common across industry. However, to the best of my knowledge, this is a somewhat small probability event. I shall describe what appears to be innovative and novel, and explain how it came about, what was the expressed logic (expressed to us researchers, of course, in a post-facto manner). For the sake of convenience, I will discuss the innovations by company and later present them grouped in certain categories.

Sun

Sun started as a single therapy formulation company, added two other therapies almost after a decade, added a surprisingly (surprising for a company of that size in 1992) expensive R&D and then went on a buying spree, acquiring companies after it had a major success in its IPO. Sun today has its formidable position due to its innovative product choice and marketing practices. The position as a speciality drug company enabled it to manage its marketing with a relatively smaller salesforce focusing on specialists. This position was further strengthened by its unique corporate position as a company, which stood a class apart from others.

While Sun did follow the usual promotion practices of offering useful gifts and services to medical practitioners, it created an image for itself as a company that was deeply interested in its therapy in scientific terms. This it did in the following ways:

- It contributed a great deal towards upgrading the knowledge of the profession through its continuing education programme.

- It helped many to stay current with the latest advances in their field by the unique gifts of monographs, books and journals.
- Further, it also contributed such literature to libraries of colleges so that it was in a position to create a favourable image among the new entrants to the profession.
- By constant monitoring of the developments in the therapy, Sun developed a system of identifying the felt needs of the medical professionals and searching for molecules that met that need. This way, it was able to keep a flow of amazingly regular new product introductions.
- To top it all, it was a remarkably bold decision for a company of its size to take up serious process and product development.

The company came to take these innovative steps as it was searching for cost effective ways of marketing their products. The basic question was in what manner could a small company, which did not possess the same reputation for technical expertise or marketing strengths as a large multinational company with which it must compete, do so. Why should its products be prescribed by leading professionals of medical specialities? Why should the specialists take the salesmen seriously at all? How could the company create a special position for itself? Dilip Shanghvi grappled with these questions himself along with the members of his marketing team. He had, as he recalls, a lot of time when the company was small, but little money. He used this time knowing the therapies, knowing the doctors, discussing with some of his friends in the medical profession about how to do these things, in learning about issues and problems. The strategy of focusing on a single therapy for compact and more efficient operations maintaining better contacts with practitioners thus emerged. So did the strategy of keeping therapy-wise marketing divisions to continue to enjoy the same advantage even when the company had become multi-therapy medicine marketer.

DRL

The history of DRL is colourful and reveals lively and dynamic, if at times less than entirely worth emulating, management. A very accomplished technocrat set up the first venture, took bold financial decisions and made it modestly successful. Then he joined hands with an aggressive partner. The remarkable recognition of the group's technical competence (an award of national significance for technical innovation) was succeeded by its opportunistic use by both the partners for collecting money from the market. Of course DRL made it big while the partner fell by the wayside primarily because he lacked the technical abilities of DRL.

- Dr Reddy achieved early successes by introducing drugs not hitherto made in this country and which were outside the scope of the DPCO. This very strategy helped DRL later with Methyldopa and with Quinolones.
- For significant periods of time, DRL focused on making bulk drugs and marketing these as an intermediate to formulators *at prices much lower than imported drugs*. This helped expand the market for the medicines and thus for them.
- Finally, by devoting significant efforts to R&D for evolving molecules, DRL has opened up a whole new vista for its future developments.

DRL came to these innovations because of the very qualities of the founder. He has the acumen for developing products and technologies, of hiring the right people who can do the relevant research and of creating organisational mechanisms for fostering this spirit of innovations. As early as in 1984, when DRL as we know it today did not even exist, he had expressed his views on why research is critical to pharma industry and how can it systematically be fostered. He opportunistically used business partners whose business interests were merely commercial but focused himself on technology and product development.

Orchid

Orchid was set up as an EOU and focused its attention on marketing cephalosporins, a class of drugs which were not really new but had a lot of growth left in them, particularly in the East Asian market. Orchid grew by focusing on that product alone, by undertaking systematic market developments for its marketing and also by achieving technical expertise in its manufacture. It expanded its production facilities quickly. It innovated by

- focusing on continuous process monitoring and improvement as well as on ensuring high quality of utilities and services to the manufacturing facilities
- focusing on cost control by instituting advanced technical as well as management control systems
- setting up a zero-effluent plant and becoming a model industrial undertaking in an industry beset with potential problems on the pollution front
- instituting an innovative water recycling facility and thus reducing its net water demand in a water scarce area

These innovations were in a sense necessary for its survival. Being in a commodity-like business, it had to get a handle on the costs and processing efficiencies for becoming competitive. The plant being located in a hopelessly water-short area, the need for water recycling was indicated if they had to obviate the messy logistics of bringing water in tankers for running the plants. Water recycling and ETP were mutually reinforcing activities. The company's uniqueness lay in putting its money where its mouth was, in investing substantial chunks of money in the activities routinely delegated to fifth priority by most of the pharma manufacturing sector. It so happened that the plant is located next to the Sterlite factory which had been forcibly closed for pollution control, this fate underscoring the economic sagacity of Orchid's investment decisions pertaining to ETP at least retrospectively.

Biocon

The very starting of a manufacturing enterprise by Kiran Muzumdar is uncommon, considering that few women-initiated enterprises have seen the light of public recognition. But that aside, Biocon grew by very quickly growing out of what Muzumdar calls the 'uninspiring low technology isinglass business' and starting the fermentation line for isolating enzymes. It is facile to underplay, as some of my academic colleagues do, the success of the company attributing it to a series of foreign collaboration, etc., but there are significant achievements to its credit. This was followed up by researching and developing applications for a number of enzymes. Biocon's noteworthy innovations include

- emphasising on significant product and applications R&D even when the company was tiny
- starting a contract R&D firm
- undertaking a systematic search and collection of tropical micro-organisms for developing a biodiversity programme on its own initiative (they collect, classify and catalogue thousands of these micro-organisms and study them for potential future commercial exploitation)
- offering an employees' stock-option policy for retaining high calibre research and other technical manpower

It would appear that these innovative activities are interrelated. For instance, enzymes are metabolites (produced during the metabolasis of tiny bugs). Hence if one systematically looked at bugs and then experimented with them for the kind of enzymes they produced, they could find a rich source of potentially saleable products. The enzyme itself is a natural product, known and classed possibly decades ago and hence non-patentable, but the process of producing it in a standardised manner is patentable and research in it therefore potentially profitable. Starting one's own research or doing it on contract for someone else adds to the total stock of knowledge and expertise of the company, and is mutually feeding. Finally, one just cannot hire exceptionally qualified researchers and expect them to produce potential commercial goldmines without giving them a share in the potential profits, and this is how ESOP came about.

Mastek

Mastek started by developing custom-made applications software, introduced software packages such as FINAC, established a nation-wide marketing set-up to push these, withdrew from them and became the franchisee to market and apply Ingress in the country, and then started looking at foreign markets. There too it went around in a manner different than others. Mastek innovated by

- introducing, marketing and customer servicing of software packages from the mid-1980s
- developing the 'wholly owned subsidiary in the host country' route in so far as exports are concerned
- developing the 'software factory' model of organisation design for catering to the software orders won by subsidiaries.

The underlying logic behind all these steps seems to be the realisation that it does one thing very well and that is providing customised software solutions backed up by reliable service. The company is mainly in customised software development but when desktops started appearing on the scene, it introduced packages as a way of expanding its reach. It then set up branches in different cities in the country to market and service the customers of these canned packages. The logic behind establishing own subsidiaries in host countries is also based on making service and response times a competitive weapon. Finally, the 'software factory' structure is merely a structural response to a situation where a number of offshore subsidiaries secure projects that need to be executed in India and hence compete for the same pool of software development engineers.

Praj

Praj went through an elaborate search for products and activities before it zeroed in on continuous fermentation plants as its area of specialisation. Later it expanded its scope to cover effluent treatment plants and heat exchange equipments in food and pharma sector. While it developed unique strengths in the first line, the latter emerged more as a part of efforts to widen the product line. The innovations perceived in Praj's case were mainly the following:

- The whole approach of 'one-stop shop' for continuous fermentation plants was novel and unique. Praj took upon itself the task of getting approvals, clearances and even financial tie-ups for the projects for which its formal responsibility was to be an engineering consultant. It handled commissioning of equipment as well, but its main job was in bringing in, adapting and applying newly developed technology.
- It set up an R&D centre for the Ethanol industry.
- The company commissioned the plants and later evolved a continuous fermentation process for making alcohol from sorghum.

Praj developed the one-stop shop concept for distilleries primarily to gain acceptance and orders in the face of competition from a more established and reputed multinational. The establishment of an R&D lab was to strengthen its technical capability and came as a step necessary to enhance its chances in competing for projects in other tropical countries.

Sumangal

- Sumangal's innovative management started from the very concept of the product. There was no almanac-cum-calendar in the country before and *Kalnirnaya* became the first product.
- Second, the innovation also lay in continuous product development and value addition, including using the

backside of the calendar for a variety of printed information: humour, literature and recipes.
- The most important move by the management was to acquire for its product a uniquely ethnic touch by which it became a virtual necessity for every Maharashtrian household.

In fact, these acts are at the very core of Sumangal's commercial success.

V-Guard

V-Guard made voltage stabilisers and for marketing these, used the dealers selling white goods. The company thus piggyrode on the growth of white goods and in particular the refrigeration market

- The innovative management practice was in development of the manufacturing system based on almost complete decentralisation.
- The company evolved mechanisms for standardising the product and instituting tough quality checks consistent with its product quality expectations.

The labour trouble in its own factory prompted the company to sell subcontracted products and this needed innovations in managing quality as well as logistics of a subcontracted manufacturing system.

Sudha

Sudha integrated vertically from being a mere RB processor to developing products and by-products based on rice bran oil. It developed innovative management practices in terms of development of

- procurement information and broker network which ensured an almost year-round supply of bran
- a bran use system which ensured the highest recovery and financial yield from a given quality of bran

- a management philosophy which focused on efficient processing rather than shrewd commercial operations as is the wont in oil seeds and oils line

Ashima

Chintanbhai collaborated initially with Sanjay Lalbhai in starting Ashima. However, when the company faced unscrupulous competition from small firms involved in texturising of polyester yarn, it decided to come out of the particular business. After parting ways with Lalbhai, Chintanbhai concentrated on the manufacture of cotton textiles.

- The group has been successful in taking over sick units (beginning with Mihir Mills of Mafatlal's), scrapping the old labour-intensive machinery and integrating the usable existing facilities with its modern plant (capital intensive).
- Its focus is on large-volume business. One of the best denim manufacturing facilities was created through imported machineries. The printing facilities were not added since such an addition of facility would have been a stumbling block to the scale of operation that Ashima wanted to achieve.
- It concentrated on production, product quality and exports, rather than on brand building in the domestic market.
- Operational freedom to the divisional heads, even in the purchase decisions (unheard in cotton textile business) along with a dual reporting system resulted in better planning and coordination at the group level and better execution at the operational and implementation stages.
- Ashima avoided selling the intermediate or semi-finished product and focused on value addition to its in-house products.

10

Strategies Adopted by the Successful Companies

Understanding Strategy

I have so far analysed decisions taken by successful companies that began as small industries, in fields as diverse as marketing, finance, manufacturing and logistics. In this chapter, I will look at the overall strategies adopted by these companies. By the word 'strategy', I mean the marshalling over of all resources of the firm to move towards its goals. The word 'strategy' has military origin and refers to a grand design within which specific configurations of forces are assigned specific targets they must deal with, using the best tactics they can devise.

When companies are small, very few declare what their strategies are and instead set about implementing them. Statements of strategies are thus not given by the successful companies, but my reconstruction uses the data on their decisions on diverse topics and on their style of functioning. It is not necessary that the companies agree with my reconstruction. In fact, their agreement does not really matter. Often a series of incremental decisions leads to growth or otherwise. The post-facto analyses of these decisions by company management are likely to be coloured by hindsight as well as by a desire to put up a front. Hence I feel that an objective view of an outsider is as reliable as any.

In a conventional method of looking at strategies, one looks at that part of the company's history which caused the growth and helped the management to transit to medium- or large-industry status. One may ignore the 'pre-industrial maturity' dabbling of the management but focus on the business for which they later became known. Analyses of strategies are hung on the following conventional pegs:

- *Product market posture:* This describes what products is the focal firm engaged in making, for which markets and for what end uses. This is a way of defining what business the firm is in.
- *Growth vector:* This describes how the firm proposes to/ actually achieves growth; by choosing which of the following 'cells'

	Old Products	New Products
Old Market	Penetration	Widening
New Market	Repositioning or geo-expansion	Diversification

Diversification is further split into related or unrelated diversification depending upon the extent of tangible relationship between the old and new business.

- *Competitive edge developed:* This describes the specific strengths or abilities of the firm to compete in its chosen business. Classically, three types of 'competitive strategy', namely, cost position, differentiation and focus, are identified.
- *Synergy deployed:* Synergy as a concept becomes relevant only when the focal firm is engaged in more than one product line. It is defined as that ability or strength which the firm deploys in both the lines, making it easy to compete in either.

- *Perception of core competence:* The question of core competence is usually raised about firms that operate several businesses which could conceivably be quite different from each other. The fashionable advice of the day to all firms is that they must focus on their core competence and, to ensure that managerial focus is not lost, should outsource all peripheral services.
- Flirtation with new activities not in core competence: The logic and duration of such activities form an important part of any analysis of strategies.

Admittedly, some of the companies are too small for a discussion on the last two points, but observation tells us that getting engaged in hopelessly disparate businesses is one common cause of stagnation in small industry in the country. Readers should be interested in trying to figure out the extent to which even successful small industries allow their managerial focus to dilute. Finally, I will also look at changes in the organisation structure of the companies reflecting the strategic shifts, if and when. Each of these strategic issues is discussed for each company, followed by an attempt to identify the commonalties in business strategies.

I will then move on to draw inferences on commonalties in other areas of decision making, as described and analysed in earlier chapters. These will cover marketing, finance, manufacturing and logistics, innovations and organisational management. Finally the commonalities will be summarised and made sense of. I will conclude by asking the central question about what we have learnt from successful companies.

Product Market Posture

Sun decided to offer 'speciality drugs' in select fields. It began by offering drugs in psychotherapy. For several years it restricted itself to that. Then it added drugs to be used in cardiovascular therapy, and in treating intestinal maladies. More recently, it offered life-saving products required in critical care. All Sun products are thus ethical drugs, prescribed by specialists to patients and in most cases (except in critical care) needed by them on a regular, long-term basis. Thus Sun's product market posture can be described thus: 'The company offers drugs used in select special fields, required by patients for a long-term treatment and prescribed by medical specialists.'

DRL marketed for much of the initial period bulk drugs needed to make ethical drugs. The choice of products was not made either on therapy or on proprietary knowledge of some kind, but on three criteria that were somewhat collateral to product or applications. These pertained to the drugs being (a) imported till DRL began making them, (b) out of the purview of Drug Price Control Order and (c) possible to be made by process modifications which would stand the test of Indian Patents Act. Thus the product market posture can be summarised as: 'DRL sold ethical drugs new to India. The company preferred to introduce the drug as a bulk drug and encouraged other Indian formulators to market the drug at prices much lower than that of the imported product, thus expanding the market.'

Biocon's product market posture has been '(fermentation-based) enzymes produced and sold as industrial intermediaries'. The company began with brewery industry, moved to fruit processing, dairy, textile and other applications, but remained with enzymes as industrial intermediaries.

Orchid decided its product market posture unambiguously. It sold Cephalosporin bulk drugs to formulators, wishing to offer its complete range in all forms, but that is what it would restrict itself to.

The product market posture of Mastek has been changing over a period of time. To begin with, it offered custom-made applications software on the clients' computers. Then it moved towards marketing standardised, canned packages. Then it marketed a platform and developed customised RDBMS applications on it. Simultaneously it also went back to applications software for foreign customers.

Sudha, like Orchid and Biocon, had a sharp definition of product market posture: 'everything in rice bran derivatives, to be sold as industrial intermediaries'. Sudha sold crude RBO to soap makers; crude, refined as well as partially hydrogenated RBO to vanaspati makers; rice bran meal to feed mixers; and fatty acid distillates such as glycerides and RB fatty acid to various industrial users. Nothing other than this was attempted or sold. It did hire out its facilities to Soya processors, but did not enter that business on its own account.

The product market posture of V-Guard had been sharp for a decade: 'a protective accessory to electrical equipment in households and small businesses'. The company in fact piggyrode on the distribution network of refrigerators and such other products. Later, V-Guard shifted from this definition of the business, remaining in electrical goods but without this sharpness of definition of business. However, 94 per cent of its sales still come from stabilisers.

Praj started as a one-stop shop for distillery units using molasses as feed stock, though its own core activities were design, erection and commissioning of complete distillery projects. Then it moved on to offering complete project engineering services, fermentation processes for ethanol production being its main line. Later, after addition of ETP, heat exchangers and such other equipment, the company has become a project engineering company for food and pharma industry.

For almost its entire lifespan, Sumangal's product market posture has been symbolised by the jingle whose last line *bhintivari kalnirnaya asawe* means that every Maharashtrian household must have the company's calendar on one of its walls. Thus its product market posture for decades has been 'ethnic almanac-cum-calendar for common households'. As printing capacity offered scope to take up job work, that activity began in a fairly non-descript way. Later, it offered commercenet services and dabbled into organising exhibitions under 'Advantage Maharashtra', etc.

Ashima had a clear definition of the product market posture. It focused exclusively on cotton fabric as an industrial intermediary. No diversification in other, man-made fibres was contemplated. Products such as denim, spinfabric and knitwear were added in quick succession in order to make Ashima a single-stop company for cotton products.

From the above discussion, it can be seen that a majority of the companies (six) have had a sharply defined product market posture throughout their life till date. Further, two more focused on a sharp product market posture after dabbling in several lines. Only two picked up activities wholly unrelated to the original product market posture at any time. Thus, clearly defined product market posture seems to be a major commonality of successful companies.

Growth Vector

Sun moved from 'therapy to therapy', that is it retained the same basic option of speciality medicines but for growth chose a different speciality. This was distinctly a form of widening the product line in the broad ethical drug field. With the establishment of its R&D laboratory, the company also introduced new products in each speciality, further strengthening its presence in each therapy. Finally, it started marketing bulk drugs as well, and this appears to be an unrelated diversification. (It is not clear whether the company marketed the very bulk drugs it also used in its own formulations, i.e., whether this was merely a way of using up the full capacity of its bulk drugs units). There was of course the business of exports. Thus the growth vector was a combination of product line widening, vertical integration and geographical expansion.

DRL's growth has come primarily by way of choosing a new drug when competition made manufacture of the earlier bulk drug unremunerative. Thus it kept on widening the product line. It also dumped earlier products if and when they became unprofitable. In the mid-1980s it started selling formulations and thus went into a sort of repositioning of the main product. For every product almost into the 1990s, it looked at market expansion as the major way of growing. The growth vector was thus a combination of penetration, product widening and vertical integration.

The growth vector identified by Biocon since the late 1970s was widening of the product line, that is, developing more applications of enzymes and producing these for the specific industrial application for which they were designed. The company became a globally significant player by sticking to this sharply defined product range.

Orchid's history is short but so far the growth vector has been one of market penetration (trying to enter every possible export market for Cephalosporin) and product range widening (e.g. sterile as well as oral products, ACA, ADCA, etc.).

Mastek has sought growth largely by geographic expansion of its market and by widening of its product line.

Sudha has grown mainly by vertical (forward) integration and hence by marketing products derived from RBO. This follows the classical Thompsonian proposition that organisations employing long-linked technologies grow by vertical integration. It did not attempt backward integration because that entailed rice milling, the parameters in which were very different from that in RB business.

Most of V-Guard's growth has come through deeper market penetration following geographic expansion from Kochi to all the South Indian cities. After a decade of its existence, the company flirted with marketing quartz watches, which project did not work out. Between 1992 and 1997, the company tried rosewood clocks as gift items, monoblock pumps and a range of electric goods (water heaters, inverters, UPS for computers, cables, etc.). Thus it tried growth by widening its product line.

Sumangal grew by deeper market penetration, first in all Marathi-speaking households and then by offering compatible ethnic almanac-cum-calendar to people speaking other languages. Thus the product was basically extended. Internet services, exhibitions, etc., were unrelated add-ons.

Praj grew first by market penetration, building distilleries for a lot of spirited coop sugar mills, and then by adding on product lines (different kinds of erection and commissioning works). Thus market penetration and widening of product lines has been its way of growing. A small part of the growth occurred by taking up manufacture of heat exchangers.

Ashima started by making denims. The company grew by first building up strengths in production and manufacture of quality products. It thus expanded by market penetration and geographic expansion. It also added lines other than denim. After 1995, it began building the retail and distribution network in the domestic market and finally entered ready-to-stitch and ready-to-wear ranges.

In summary, it can be said that vertical integration as a strategy of growth is not a common feature of successful companies. Sudha was the only company which grew that way right from the start. Sun, Praj and DRL took to vertical integration some time during their life, though after they had established their business on sound footing. The most common ways of growth were through market penetration, geographic expansion of markets and widening the product line, in that order.

Competitive Edge Developed

Sun developed its competitive edge by two distinct means. One was creating a corporate image in the minds of the prescribing doctors. This was done through a series of steps described earlier. The second advantage was developed by continuous efforts at new products introduction, for which the company kept a panel of doctors who recommended a new drug, assisted in its testing and release, etc. After its IPO, Sun also used its surplus liquidity as a competitive edge in buying up or acquiring controlling interests in pharma companies which gave it the advantage of low cost and speedy expansion of its manufacturing base.

DRL's competitive advantage flowed from the technical expertise of Anji Reddy, and manifested itself in its uncanny skill of identifying products hitherto not made in the country but having a huge domestic market. It enjoyed a price advantage in every product thus introduced.

Biocon developed the image of a scientifically sound company which develops its own processes for manufacture of the enzyme and also stays with the user through the stages of applications. This complete reliability in technical servicing worked as a competitive edge for the company.

In Orchid's case, superior position on costs by working on process efficiencies and yields, and maintaining an impeccable quality standard to the point where the company became a benchmark for comparing others' products were the two competitive advantages.

The original entrepreneurs in Mastek all came from a trained management background and thus had a comparative advantage of being able to better appreciate the management processes sought to be supported by their software. The very name of their group was 'Management And Software Technical Consultants'. Throughout its history, Mastek has used its ability to offer 'management-friendly' software support and this possibly distinguishes it from other software companies.

Sudha's ability to source RB almost year round, to sort out RB by quality and to design organisational routines for the most optimal utilisation of any given RB lot was its basic competitive advantage. Its ability to improve processing efficiency through bootstrapping was another.

The initial competitive advantage of V-Guard was in terms of superior product attributes (low-high voltage cut-off, i.e., stepping up or down the voltage to the desired level and automatic cut-off when limits were crossed). The company then developed an edge in distribution. Finally, when the volumes rose, it developed the ability to manage subcontracted manufacture with consistent and high quality as its competitive advantage.

Initially, Praj's competitive edge was in understanding the labyrinthine process of new projects in the cooperative sugar sector and offering 'one-stop shop' project services for distilleries. The social contacts of the entrepreneur came in handy here. Later, superior engineering technology and ability to commission projects became its competitive advantages.

For its core business, developing a close identity with the culture and the way of life of the urban middle class Maharashtrian populace was Sumangal's competitive advantage.

Ashima consolidated on the strength of quality consistency and timely delivery of the products to the garment manufacturer. It later developed an understanding of the buyers' requirements and developed a system where their specifications could be quickly translated into production.

In summary of the 10 cases observed, the most common feature of successful companies is that they relied on their knowledge and expertise for efficient management of the manufacturing process or on technology as the chief competitive weapon. They developed such an advantage when none previously existed. The second common source of a competitive edge was developed in product quality and consistency. Cultivating and establishing a close rapport with the crucial elements of DMUs (doctors in case of Sun, cooperative boards for Praj) through innovative and much-needed professional services and support was the source of the competitive edge for two companies. Two more used low-cost profiles developed through technology or process expertise as a competitive edge.

Synergy Deployed

The experience developed in garnering market share in a selected speciality therapy by focused efforts of promotion among specialists of that therapy was the chief synergy used by Sun among its products. Its corporate image in the medical fraternity helped. Its expertise in identifying opportunities for new product introductions can be termed a second synergy between products and the line in which Sun entered.

Understanding the pharma-chemistry and the process of manufacture has been the main source of synergies between diverse products which DRL made. In the formulations market, the corporate image became the only synergy.

Research capability and the ability to evolve applications was the synergy deployed between diverse products developed by Biocon. The product line of Mastek has not been changed so significantly as to require a discussion regarding synergy. The ability to manage continuous processing for long-chain fatty acids was Sudha's main synergy across products.

The only sources of synergy one can attribute to V-Guard's attempts to diversify in unrelated products would be (a) its ability to manage sourcing of products made at third party locations and (b) its access to distribution networks. In Praj's case, the ability to manage projects was the synergy deployed among different product lines.

Sumangal's synergy across extended products (almanaccum-calendars in other languages) was in terms of printing facilities. Between the calendar and its commercenet-related services there was no synergy.

For Ashima, knowledge of buyer behaviour in the garment industry was one source of synergy. Expertise on high-volume manufacture with reduced process costs and high efficiencies was the second synergy across different fabric lines.

Summarising, it can be said that seven of the 10 companies studied had product lines sufficiently different as to make the concept of synergy relevant. The most common attempts were to derive synergy out of the manufacturing or operating technology (in six out of the seven cases). By 'operating technology', we refer to a learnt and developed organisational routine for certain operations.

Thus Sun had developed organisational expertise in

- identifying the need for a particular medicine felt by medical fraternity
- identifying through its advisory panel a suitable molecule for meeting the need
- developing and testing the relevant formulation and introducing it well before anyone else
- promoting it among a select group of specialists

This is operating technology so far as we are concerned.

Corporate or product brand equity was deployed as a synergy by two companies while two others tried to use distribution muscle as a source of synergy.

Perception of Core Competence

Sun perceives its core competence in marketing of high-quality drugs needed in long-term treatment of select diseases. It also uses its competence in new product introduction. DRL perceives its expertise in pharma-chemistry and the ability to translate laboratory-level processes to manufacturing plant as its core competence.

Biocon's perception of its core competence was stated by one senior executive, 'We understand and can manage fermentation for making enzymes.' That is one reason the company did not enter the 'commodity-like' business of making antibiotics though that too involved managing basically a biochemical process. At Orchid, an understanding of the chemistry and the knowledge of how to control the process of making the product has been viewed as the core competence of the company.

Mastek has zeroed in on its understanding of management processes and its ability to develop software solutions for supporting these processes as its core competence. That is how, despite massive demands, the company did not enter businesses such as share registry or computer education, as several of their contemporaries did.

'We know rice bran processing and rice bran oil trade. We know the people who use RBO and its derivatives' was the way core competence was defined at Sudha. It refused so much as even an attempt to enter consumer marketing of RB oil since that strayed away from its core competence.

Control on quality of products assembled from electronic components was the core competence at V-Guard. The second core competence was in marketing of consumer durables, in particular electrical goods.

Process engineering design and detailed engineering of projects were the original competencies developed by Praj. Spotting, taking up and absorbing new technology, undertaking own process engineering, R&D and use of IT as a strategic tool in project engineering supplemented the core competence of the company.

The core competence of Sumangal certainly lay in knowing the pulse of the urban Maharashtrian populace as well as in organising large-scale manufacture and distribution of the product. Ashima seems to have developed the perception of its core competence in conversion of cotton into fabrics of different types.

Clearly then, the most commonly held core competence was in the field of manufacturing of the chosen product line. This was in terms of understanding a certain process, bootstrapping on it for achieving process efficiencies as well as superior quality of the product, and extending it. The other areas in which companies developed core competencies were in the skill of identifying a product and/or technology for making it and commercialising its manufacture. This was thus a skill of sort of institutionalised, structured innovation and technology absorption.

Logic and Duration of Flirtation with New Activities not in Core Competence

Sun has virtually never strayed from areas of its core competence. Only recently has it entered drugs needed for immediate rather than long-term treatment, but this is a minor digression (if one were to consider it as such) from its consistent stand. The marketing of bulk drugs undertaken by it is possibly of the nature of using up the slack in production facilities.

DRL has been straying from its core competence for almost 17 years, since Anji Reddy's first unit (lease finance, computer peripherals, halogen lamps,...). These have been purely opportunistic moves, often targeted at garnering investments from the public and at times prompted by a combination of tax planning and speculative motive. Anji Reddy recognises these for what they are and does not justify them. He is clear that in future the company will stick to its area of core competence.

For V-Guard, the logic of entry in unrelated product lines can only be to exploit the access to the distribution network. The company regrets not having ventured into constant voltage transformers at the time of the computer boom, even though this product has great commonality with a common stabiliser. The company continues to experiment with new unrelated products, as it possibly perceives its competence in marketing.

Sumangal went in for commercenet service because it was easier to reach the thousands of Maharashtrian families abroad electronically. It took a site on India.world and put a 45-day calendar on it to begin with. The response was overwhelming as people used it for identifying *muhurats* (auspicious occasions for undertaking any major event). The company experimented more with offering different kinds of information about Maharashtra and found that people appreciated this. Finally it decided to take a site and call it Commercenet India (named like similar sites on Japan and Canada), using the data on Maharashtra likely to be useful to marketers and entrepreneurs, and using the site to put out advertisements. This business is small but expected to grow.

Chintan Parikh, the man behind Ashima, played around a lot before Ashima. But he stopped flirting with the other lines of business as soon as Ashima Syntex reoriented its business (into cotton). With reducing focus on the other lines, even Knackmo, a machinery division, was integrated into Ashima's mainline. Biocon, Orchid, Sudha, Praj and Mastek have not strayed at all from the area of their core competence.

Six of the 10 companies studied did not allow their focus on chosen business line to dilute at all. Two companies batted around in a wide range of activities either to experiment with them or for speculative reasons before choosing a focus and settling down to it. V-Guard and Sumangal allowed this focus to be diluted after succeeding in the chosen area and achieving stability in it. This was done for different reasons, most possibly as the scope for further business growth in the original line was seen to be limited

Changes in Organisation Structure as Reflecting the Strategic Shifts

Sun was organised on functional lines to start with. It underwent reorganisation at least in its marketing set-up when it became a multi-therapy company. Marketing function is now organised into four divisions, each handling a certain specified product group. This was done to achieve focus. Overall the organisation seems to be in a state of flux and the structural response to the series of acquisitions is anything but complete.

DRL is organised on functional lines. Dr Reddy has followed the system of floating separate firms rather than starting activities in the same firm and then reorganising them in SBUs, etc. As such, DRL had not gone through any major reorganisation till 1994. In that year, it decided to merge the various formulations marketing divisions in one, to achieve greater economy in the use of resources.

Orchid is organised on functional lines and has not undergone any reorganisation. Biocon also multiplied the number of firms in the group. The company did not mention any significant reorganisation but it must be stated that once its first 'large-volumes' company Helix goes on stream, there could be a reorganisation. The current organisation is functional.

Mastek went through a major reorganisation to support its growing overseas business. Offshore factories of the overseas subsidiaries were created in the India office to better service them with software production support. This followed the company decision to shift from overseas project administration model to overseas subsidiary model of organisational form.

Sudha has always been a tidy, functionally organised and tightly controlled organisation. As the new line got added to Praj, core teams who had expertise in the new lines formed 'industry groups' supported by the common pool of engineers, in design, purchase, fabrication and erection. This reorganisation occurred in 1995–96.

Ashima's reorganisation primarily involved consolidation and organisation on divisional lines. Ashima Fabrics focuses on assorted fabrics such as poplins, satins, twills, oxford and lining materials. Ashima Denims focuses on indigo denim cloth. Spinfab focuses on high-value dyed cotton fabrics. There are SBUs for denim, spin fabric and knitwear. SBUs are looked after by the COO who has the overall responsibility, from securing orders to executing them.

Not surprisingly (considering that they are just emerging into medium/large company size and scope), more of the successful companies maintained a functional form of organisation with varying degrees of formalisation. Some became organised on product basis in so far as marketing was concerned but remained functional in the overall sense. (That is, overall the organisation was organised on functional lines but the internal organisation of marketing comprised groups focusing on a chosen product set.) Ashima had a dual reporting structure with the SBU concept emerging as the dominant structural response to its expanding business. Mastek had organised itself on market basis: barring common services, most of the groupings in the organisation were organised around a chosen set of clientele.

The entire discussion above is summarised in the table below:

TABLE 10.1
Summary of Strategic Choices Made by the Successful Companies

Name	Product Market Posture	Growth Vector	Competitive Edge	Synergy	Core Competence	Dilution of Focus	Organisation
Sun	1	2, 3	2, 3	1, 3	2		Product/Functional
DRL	4	1, 2, 3, 4	1, 6	1	2	**	Functional
Orchid	1	1, 4, 2	1, 2		1		Functional
Biocon	1	1, 2	1, 5	1	1		Functional
Sudha	1	4	1, 7		1		Functional
Mastek	1	1, 2, 3	1	1	2		Market driven
V-Guard	2	1, 2, 3, 5	4, 2	2, 3	3	10	Functional
Praj	1	1, 3, 4	3, 1	1	2		Product
Sumangal	2	1, 2, 5	5		3	21	Product
Ashima	4	1, 2, 3	1, 6	1	1	**	Product

(continued)

Table 10.1 (continued)

The numbers indicate behaviour described below:

Product Market Posture

1. Sharp definition, finely focusing the business initially for several years and then gradually expanding the product market coverage in related products
2. Sharp definition of product market posture for several years and then choosing an unrelated product
3. Opportunistically defined product market posture with varying product specifics
4. Trying out many things, zeroing in on one sharp focus and then expanding

Growth Vector

1. Market penetration
2. Geographic expansion
3. Widening of product line
4. Vertical integration
5. Unrelated diversification

The numbers in the cell represent sequencing of the choices made.

Competitive Edge

1. Rooted in expertise in technology/processing efficiency
2. Rooted in product quality
3. Rooted in cultivating/knowing the critical element in the decision-making unit
4. Rooted in distribution
5. Rooted in knowing buyers' requirements very well
6. Low cost profiles
7. Rooted in knowledge of raw material supply

Synergy (attempted deployment)

1. Derived from technology
2. Derived from distribution muscle
3. Derived from brand name/corporate image

Core Competence (perceived by management/inferred by analyst)

1. Managing a specific configuration of manufacturing facilities
2. Product/technology identification and commercialisation
3. Distribution

(continued)

Table 10.1 (continued)

Dilution of focus

Years represent the number of years since establishment (of the focus) when focus was lost, if at all
Blank represents no loss of focus at all
** Represents strong establishment of focus after engaging in a variety of unrelated businesses

Organisation

Product: organisation is by products, and for each product, functions are under one command barring common services
Product/functional: marketing is organised by product groups but the rest of the organisation is on functional lines
Functional: organisation is arranged on functional lines
Market driven: markets/customer groups arrange organisation

Commonalities in Functional Management

Marketing Strategy

Table 4.1 in Chapter 4 (p. 118) reveals that most successful companies (eight) identified products/services that were at the growth stage of their life cycles. Only two entered what may be considered stable products (at the maturity stage in their PLC) whose demand was expected to grow only at demographic rates.

Seven companies used product features as their chief competitive weapons in the marketing war, four of them very emphatically so. Sumangal kept innovating and enriching its product features as competition entered, aware as it was that at no stage would it get the advantages of the Patents Act. The same was the case with Biocon, where the product enzyme cannot be patented. Orchid's products have run out of the patent restrictions and that is how it can make them and yet through sheer quality standards, it has competed in a tough international market. Distribution as an element of marketing strategy seems to be less favoured than product features. Only three companies V-Guard, Mastek and Sumangal, used distribution as a strength and a competitive weapon, though in each case the specific approach to developing it as their strength differed. V-Guard used the distribution network used by white goods (consumer electric durables) sellers. Mastek set up branches for selling its then new canned software products. Sumangal used the distribution system of the news agencies as it had extensive contacts in the newspaper world. Surprisingly, low price position, undoubtedly derived from low cost position, was a popular way of performing better in the market. Five companies used it. Some used it very emphatically indeed. Industrial intermediate makers such as DRL, Orchid, Sudha and Ashima had much stronger reason to use the low price position due to the nature of their businesses. The best use was in expanding the size of the market itself, as was done by DRL and, interestingly, by Sumangal (which sells a final rather than intermediate product).

Advertising as a weapon to success was seldom used. Nor even promotion in the BTL sense. Unique styles of promotion were used as critical elements of the marketing mix by just three companies. Thus, Sun had for its most salient element of marketing mix its remarkable style of promotion of the company as a scientifically oriented, professional company which could be trusted to come up with the latest and the best drugs. Praj used total project support as a very important tool in marketing. Sumangal was the only company that relied upon strong pull factors for selling. Truly, this is bad news for the ad man. Thus, the model successful company seems to rely on product features such as quality and consistency as its chief weapon for competing, followed by maintaining a low price profile derived from its cost profile.

In summary, choosing products in the growth phase of their respective product life cycles, relying on product features and striving for low price position were the major modes for competition associated with successful companies.

Financing Strategy

Table 5.1 in Chapter 5 (p. 139) throws up the following inferences regarding the financial management in successful companies.

Of the seven companies for whom we have enough data for analysis, six were conservative and either maintained low debt in their capital structure or reduced its proportion over the years. In one case, namely Sudha, the ratio changed dramatically in favour of debts, undoubtedly caused by large capital investments in its latest spate of diversifications. This happened after a decade of its existence. Four companies used the resources mobilised for building up current assets, two emphasised building up fixed assets while one invested similar amounts in both types of assets. The model company behaviour was to keep inventory and debtors at about the industry average. High investments in fixed assets by one company, Orchid, was compensated by its extremely tight working capital management, far more efficient than the industry norms. Debtors as a competitive tool was deployed by just one company, DRL, possibly more in defence than out of choice.

Conservatism is thus the only common thread in the financial management of successful companies. Three have demonstrated evidence of prudence and conservatism throughout their lifespan (that is, low debts, high liquidity and preference to building up current assets, if necessary, first). One company had adopted conservative financing for substantial time but changed in favour of riskier financing after they became successful, due to the need to expand investments to match growth. One, DRL, became very conservative after it became successful, after playing around with borrowed funds or funds mobilised through adventurous manner.

Manufacturing and Logistics

The following discussion is based on Table 6.1 from Chapter 6 (p. 159). Four companies took to state-of-the-art technologies in manufacturing and logistics. Four started with technologies that were nothing special, three continued in that fashion, while one started developing its own. Just two started with their own technologies. Thus inventiveness in technology is clearly not *sine qua non* of success. The model successful company started with or even maintained facilities that were not much larger than needed to meet their expectations on sales. Several in fact kept smaller capacities and used third-party manufacture. Three companies expanded their manufacturing facilities rapidly (expansion occurring in phases but in quick succession, may be once in two years or even quicker). Six were more circumspect and added facilities slowly (less than once every three to four years). One managed fairly well to match this expansion with sales growth. Thus the model behaviour was for slow expansion. Four companies emphasised bootstrapping efforts to continuously upgrade both the quality of products as well as processing efficiencies. Two reported efforts on quality but did not speak about efficiencies. Four did not elaborate on this matter at all, possibly implying that this was not critical to their success.

In summary, starting with a modest size of facilities and expanding them to match sales growth, while engaging in continuous and arduous work of bootstrapping to improve processing efficiency and better product quality are the features associated with successful companies.

Organisational Issues and Managerial Style

This section summarises my judgements on the overall organisational personality of the companies studied. These are impressionistic judgements and added to sort of complete the picture. The attributes of successful companies on several parameters related to organisational and managerial style have been presented in Table 7.1 in Chapter 7 (p. 176). As can be seen from the table, more successful small companies start with or transit to the WHC form within a decade of commencement of business. In my study, four have still not made the transition and two are perhaps suffering for it. The motivation to becoming a WHC may come from the need to garner investible resources through an IPO as in three cases or just for 'changing from the partnership mindset for achieving high growth' as in one. The change in the mindset of the entrepreneur as being very crucial for achieving high and sustained growth is in fact a singularly important lesson thrown up by this research. The reasons for not transiting to the WHC form are firmly rooted in the desire to keep control on one's empire as in three cases and the absence of financial compulsion or xenophobia.

We note that four companies (Mastek, Sun, Orchid and Praj) began as team ventures, often in sharing the risks as well, and hence were never dominated by a single individual. They found the issue of delegation to senior staff, etc., to be much less painful and have done it in most cases. Of the six cases that were individual or family ventures, four retain the same ethos of control and domination by the family and this happens despite attempts to superimpose a formal work system on the essentially star-type organisation. Systems of workflow and the extent of formalisation seem to be in a range. The trend is to move from entrepreneur-dependent and almost ad hoc towards IT-based, highly formal, documented and structured, with formal MIS and control systems such as cost centres and SBUs. But the movement seems to halt around achieving basic stability in routines and making the systems entrepreneur-independent for routine work, rather than going the whole hog in formalisation. In overall terms, the fox mode of leadership, of cautious, 'thinking and learning' stance, with participation and even team effort, seems to dominate and is being observed in six organisations. The pure lion cub mode of aggressive go-getting was seen in three, and the entrepreneur-dependent but cautious lizard mode in just one organisation. Finally, floating too many firms was a blunder committed by quite a few firms. The rationale was mainly the need to take advantage of regulatory or fiscal concessions available to small industries to be able to survive the competition.

In summary, small companies which are successful transit to the WHC form of organisations fairly early, possibly mainly to discard the 'small-industry mindset', and attempt to hire professionals. Their pioneers try and give up excessive control orientation; develop formal and structured systems of work; and emphasise teamwork, participation and organisational learning.

Innovations

The innovations reported in Chapter 9 relate to product features, manufacturing technology, operating technology or other managerial aspects. These are summarised in Table 10.2.

TABLE 10.2
Innovations in Successful Companies

Sl. No.	Name	Product	Manufacturing Technology	Operating Technology	Marketing or Other
1	Sun			Y	YY
2	DRL	Y	Y		Y
3	Orchid		Y	Y	Y
4	Mastek	Y		YY	Y
5	Biocon	Y		YY	Y
6	Sudha			YY	
7	V-Guard			YY	
8	Praj		Y	YY	Y
9	Sumangal	YY			
10	Ashima			YY	Y

A look at the table shows that none of the companies studied had zero innovations. Most typically the innovation was in the field of what we call operational technology, with as many as eight companies reporting such innovations. Innovative practices either in marketing (unique methods of promotion, etc.) or other management areas were seen in seven companies. Four companies had innovated in product features and three in logistics/manufacturing technologies.

Making Sense of These Findings

Marketing

Choosing products in the growth phase of their product life cycles is important for growth. This seems to be fairly simple to understand. When the product category is on a growth track as a whole, the players are not so concerned with fighting each other. The cake is growing and hence every one has a plateful. The market possibly offers scope for developing niches, offering special product or service features within it. So there is greater likelihood of growth.

On the other hand, if the demand for a product category as a whole is stagnant or waning, a new entrant in the small industry class is unlikely to thrive on it and become big. If the overall demand is huge but stagnant, the sort of *papad*-pickle-firecrackers-*masalas* case, then the field is likely to be quite crowded as it is. Competition is likely to be intense and possibly spread across the country with location-specific advantages. A small industrialist will have no specific advantages here except his facelessness—the wrong competitive advantage and the one that vanishes when he becomes big. Thus we may not find too many successes in products that are growing only at demographic rates.

Why do entrepreneurs opt for established products that are likely to be on a plateau in their PLC? Possibly because of the feeling of safety it offers. Others have introduced this product, they all seem to sell, and this item is something that is always going to be needed, so it is safe. (As a *marwari* businessman once expressed while talking to me, '*yeh chalnewala* item *hain*'). This is the field of the lizard entrepreneur, who wishes to cater to the simple but perennial needs of the populace and to thrive on it. Not the choice of someone who wishes to become a giant. The question of how one should go about identifying whether a product is in the growth phase or not is more complex, involving understanding of the product, business and economic trends and still requiring an appetite for some risk.

Competitive advantage is found, according to our research, in the product features and quality or in the price of the product. What is more important is that entrepreneurs do not find competitive advantage in advertising and expensive schemes for mass promotion. Promotion of a specific and unique style, like that of Sun, offers durable competitive advantage and has been tried by some.

Finance

The financial strategies do not offer a convergent message, though clearly low debt and/or reducing debt level when the firm grows is a dominant behavioural pattern. Higher levels of debt mean more leveraged business, with greater risk of going under in the event of things not going the way one wishes. While entrepreneurship involves risk taking, the choice of successful entrepreneurs is clearly in favour of moderate financial risks. This is possibly a reflection of common prudence. The second aspect to become clear is that more successful entrepreneurs follow rather than reform the industry practice on inventory and credits in so far as sales are concerned. The shift in very large companies towards making retailers pay before delivery, etc., does not seem to be reflected in the behaviour of successful companies, possibly because they are in the process of establishing themselves. The third and perhaps the most important lesson is that most successful entrepreneurs use additional resources (whether business surpluses or borrowings) first to build up current assets. Liquidity before expansion is the simple rule then. Those who flout it, quite simply, go under.

Manufacturing and Logistics

The more successful entrepreneurs keep the size of the facilities modest and expand them at a speed that matches the sales growth, but painstakingly work towards improving processing efficiencies and product quality from the same facility. They think big but act modest and do a whole lot of grease-and-grime kind of nitty-gritty work. Bootstrapping to become lean and mean; to get the best yield, the lowest material wastage, the lowest consumption of utilities; and yet to maintain uniform and high product quality is then the key to sound business. This is inevitable if entrepreneurs are to find competitive advantage in product quality, features and price, as already indicated above. The key is probably in continuous efforts to improve manufacturing and logistics.

Organisation

Entrepreneurs quickly transit to a WHC form of organisation. This is done by a rogue simply to garner money from the public through an IPO. The successful entrepreneur is not a rogue. Equally frequently, the organisation culture and style of management changes from possibly person-dependent, closed, secretive, ad hoc and peremptory, to open, transparent, team-based and formal. Most important in this is the question of hiring professionals who are encouraged to become organisation-oriented rather than burdened with the need to become personally loyal. Authority is delegated to them and they are encouraged to contribute in a knowledge-based manner to the firm's decisions. The picture of a hardworking and brilliant entrepreneur ploughing his lonely furrow is not consistent with the modern times and the business complexities it involves.

Innovations

We saw earlier that no firm had zero innovation. We had put limited meaning to the word innovation: it was not invention, but a way of doing things that is not common, not usual at all and possibly quite unique. Entrepreneurs are not inventors, though some inventors such as Anji Reddy become entrepreneurs. This statement makes eminent general sense. Starting from a position of insufficient strength and staying power, quickly transiting to medium if not large business category is possible only if the entrepreneurs leave the beaten track, do something that is their own. We have found these innovations to be most common in the operating technology and some functional management areas. The former refers to an organisational routine that is designed to achieve something that is unique to the firm. Such as Anji Reddy's skill in identifying and making drugs that till he started making them were imported and expensive. Such as Sunil Handa's skill in managing the purchase and use of medical-grade plastic in a manner that brought down the inventory costs as well as even the basic plastic cost per bottle, despite a gulf war. Such as Raja Rao's skill in developing systems for procurement of rice bran to lengthen his processing year to a surprising extent and for use of the input rice bran to get the best economic output from it. Such as Kochouseph Chittilapilly's skill in managing large volume of business in voltage stabilisers on just subcontracted manufacture. All these acts needed development of operating technologies that are innovations of the entrepreneurs concerned. Innovations in functional management are easier to understand and have been explained in the text.

Strategy

But the crux is in the commonality discovered in overall business strategy: The 'model' successful company, so to say, is characterised by a sharp definition of business right from the start. It grows first by market penetration, followed by geographic expansion and then by widening its product line. It derives its competitive advantage from its mastery over the manufacturing process or operational technology and possibly also product quality. It attempts to derive synergy from application of this facet (i.e., mastery over operational technology) and develops this as its core competence. It does not dilute the focus for quite a number of years and is functionally organised.

This is straightforward and eminently sensible!

Lessons From Success

Blundering

I am very gratified to note that seven of the eight common blunders I had identified in *How not to...* are indeed common only to sick and stagnant firms. Successful companies do not seem to commit them at all, or even if they veer around them for a while, quickly correct themselves. At the same time, I must note that floating too many firms is a common act, to be seen even in successful enterprises. It seems there are tangible benefits of doing so. Again, the act of creative accounting after floating too many firms is possibly more of a blunder than merely floating them. After all, what is of crucial importance is the need to become respectable in terms of formal asset figures and bottom line. If all the firmlets are maintained without taking recourse to creative accounting, then they could be merged at a later date to form a respectable enough firm.

Does One have to be Counter-intuitive to Succeed?

What is the formula for success everyone teaches everyone else everywhere? Hard work, frugal spending, prudent investment and consistency, about sums it up. Others might add qualities such as patience, confidence in one self and moderate risk taking. Some others usually insist upon the role of the goddess of fortune. If religiously inclined in the good old Hindu tradition, then one sees the role of *karma*, etc. I am certainly not going to state that these 10 entrepreneurs succeeded because they were lucky. Or even that they had done such marvellous good deeds in their past incarnations (though, of course, I do not mean otherwise!). Research was done to find out what specific acts seem to be associated with success and hence worth learning from. But as the title of this section asks, is it necessary that one must do counter-intuitive, strange, uncommon or seemingly crazy acts to succeed dramatically? What are these strange acts in the sample companies studied?

- A company such as Sun which has barely reached a turnover of Rs 25 crore invests a couple of crores in a research and development centre. The decision is taken by its key promoter who himself is not even a pharmacy graduate!
- A man called K.R. Rao, who comes from a middle-class upbringing, in his thirties, invests virtually every penny he earns in the Gulf to set up his company. Where is ordinary prudence?
- A bright engineer, Pramod Choudhari, who spent years cutting tools, goes around myriad government offices to see to it that his client is allowed to set up a distillery. And this he does despite offering a top-class plant and technology to the clients.
- An exceptional chemical engineer Anji Reddy goes about entertaining ideas of investment in computer peripherals and even halogen lamps even when his own pharmacy company is exceptionally successful.
- A successful manufacturer called Kochouseph Chittilapilly closes down his factory when he first hits labour trouble in Kerala (I am told, you face labour trouble in Kerala on

the very day you hire the workers!) and goes the whole hog for 100 per cent subcontracted manufacture.

The answer to this question lies in the fact that small-scale industrialists are often in a hopelessly over-constrained situation. They are in a low-level equilibrium.

> small scale of operations → little competitive strength → little returns → little strength to grow bigger

Sometimes this might become a trap, and sooner if they commit one of the more troublesome blunders. They can perhaps get out of this equilibrium (or the trap) only by choosing an unusual and unconventional set of actions. Staid and stolid small-scale industrialists who start a business on a *chalnewala* item do well for themselves in terms of making a livelihood. But they make the transition to the medium/big industry status only over generations. Hence the question that one may need to ask is how can small industries be managed successfully without taking any seemingly strange decisions? For only such decisions hold the possibility of breaking out of the small industry mould, of returns commensurate with their desire to grow and transit to medium/large industry status. Thus small industrialists need to be wary of excessive caution in operating decisions if they think there is enough justification for it. Of course, this does not wholeheartedly encourage them towards profligate and speculative financing.

Innovate or Perish

Every successful industry has done some innovative thing, though not necessarily inventive in the sense of coming up with a new product. Entrepreneurs are not inventors and you saw that only two of the 10 successful companies succeeded because of their introducing a wholly new product in the market. There is a clear difference between innovation and invention. And I am using the former word in its more diluted form, specifically connoting an unusual or uncommon decision, thing or way of working. The reason why these companies did well despite odds of a usual small enterprise in India is that they found a new method of working which got results in a critical aspect of their business surer, better or cheaper. This innovation then helps them get over the image, quality or cost problems associated with small industry. Clearly, just doing what everyone else does in every possible field is not enough. To get an edge, one has to do better. And this is done through sustained application of the mind to the business situations at hand.

Quotable Quotes

I end this book with some statements made by some successful entrepreneurs for the wisdom and value they offer to those who wish to grow big:

Kiran Mazumdar of Biocon stated, 'I started manufacturing isinglass. But soon I realised that I could not continue doing just that uninspiringly low technology work. I had to start something that was technically more challenging.'

Ashank Desai remarked about the pace of expansion of fixed assets of his company, 'Lean and mean is for me. We have always been careful and expanded only in phases, fortunately without really losing on any business.'

Pramod Choudhari of Praj stated, 'If they (customers) felt that they could rely on you to give them complete technical support, it always helped in winning them. It was Praj's turnkey approach and of course their reliability factor that brought them orders.'

About the Author

S.J. Phansalkar runs his own management consultancy firm—Amol Management Consultants, Nagpur. Prior to this, he was on the Faculty of the Institute of Rural Management, Anand, during which time he completed the Fellow Programme in Management at the Indian Institute of Management, Ahmedabad. Dr Phansalkar has undertaken consulting assignments with various small-scale enterprises, and has published several research papers, newspaper articles and management cases. He is the author of *How Not to Ruin Your Small Industry* (Response, 1996).